RECORDED VERSIONS GUITAR

AUTHENTIC TRANSCRIPTIONS WITH NOTES AND TABLATURE

John 5
Vertigo

T0052911

Art concept and photos: John 5, Mark Friedman and Chet Haun
Music transcriptions by David Stocker

ISBN 0-634-09003-8

HAL•LEONARD®
CORPORATION

7777 W. BLUEMOUND RD. P.O. BOX 13819 MILWAUKEE, WI 53213

Visit Hal Leonard Online at
www.halleonard.com

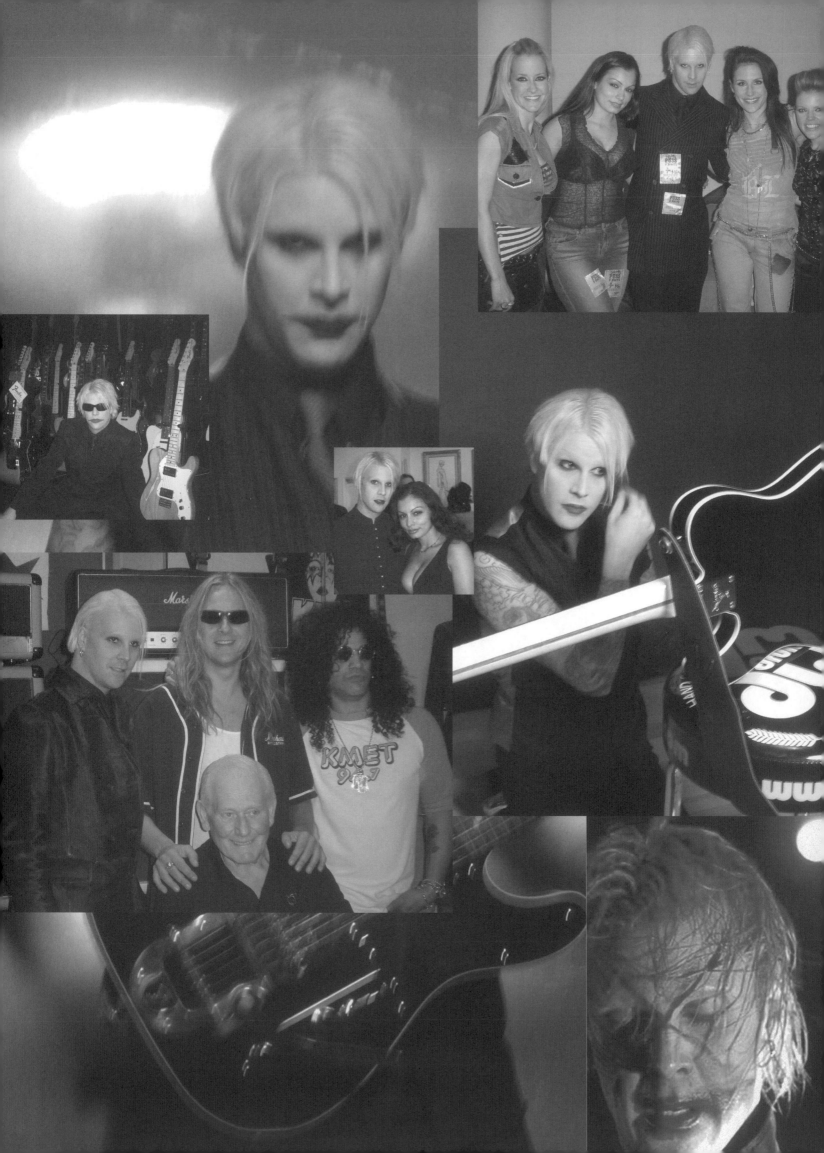

Needles, CA

Music by John 5, Kevin Savigar and J.T. Harding

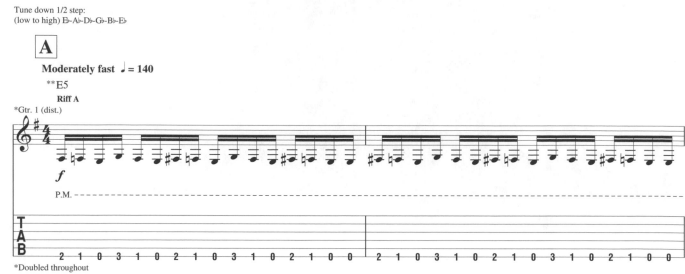

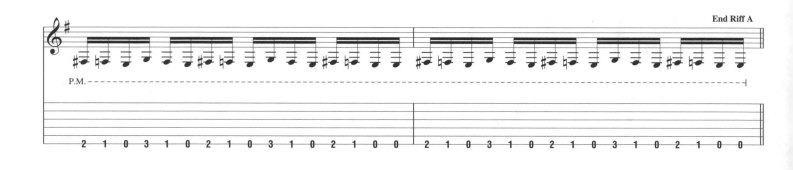

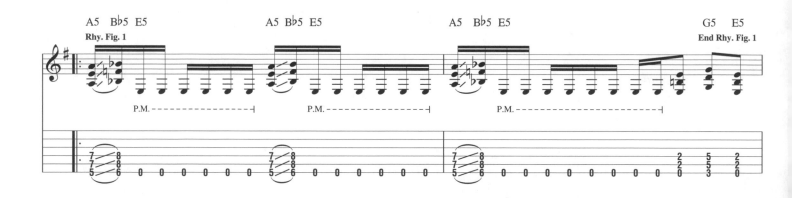

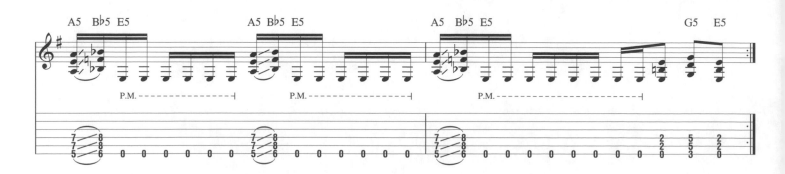

B

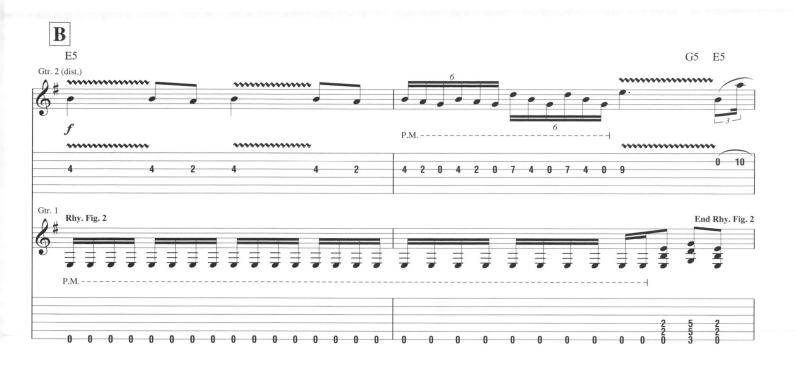

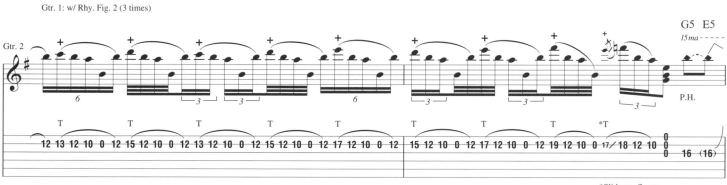

*Slide tap finger.

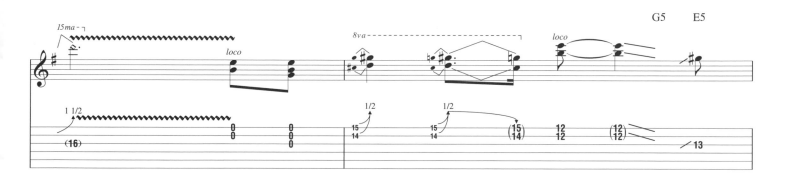

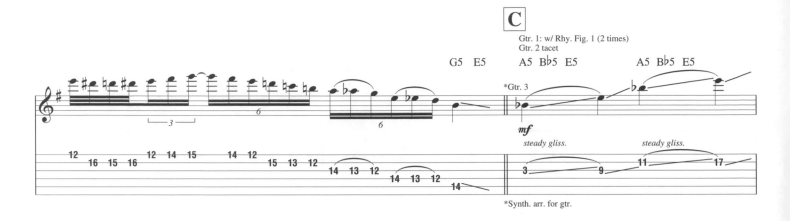

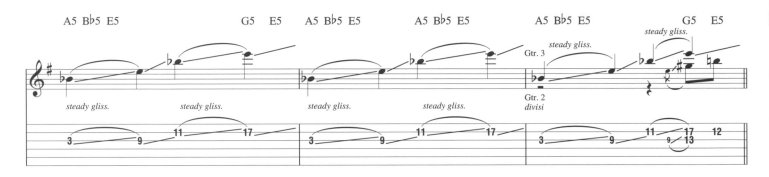

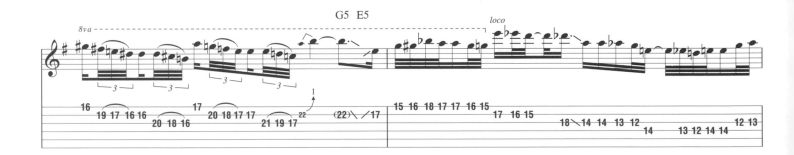

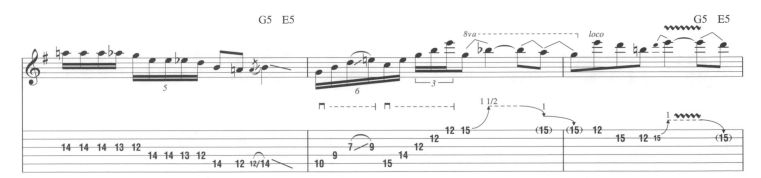

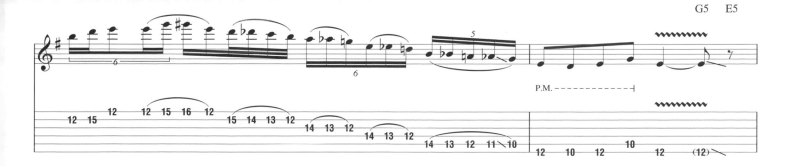

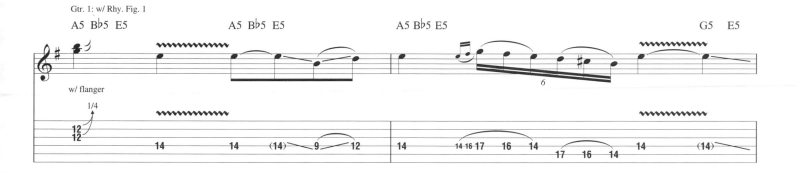

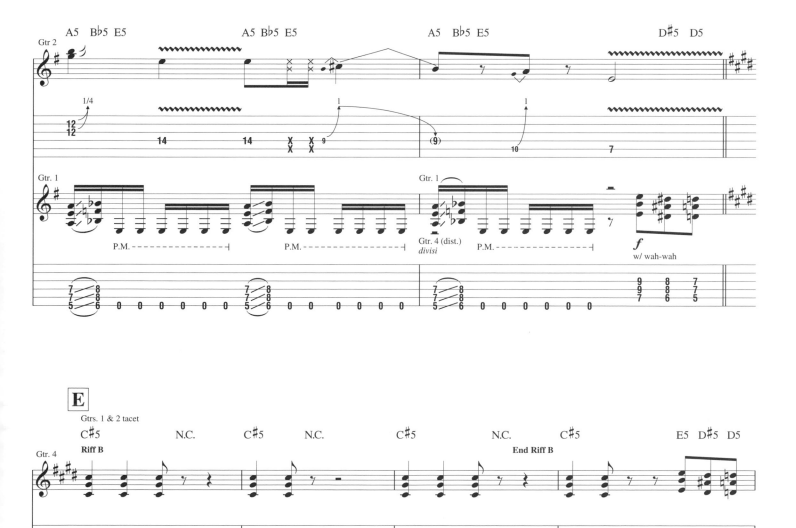

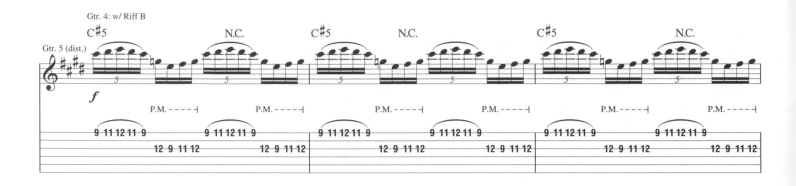

F

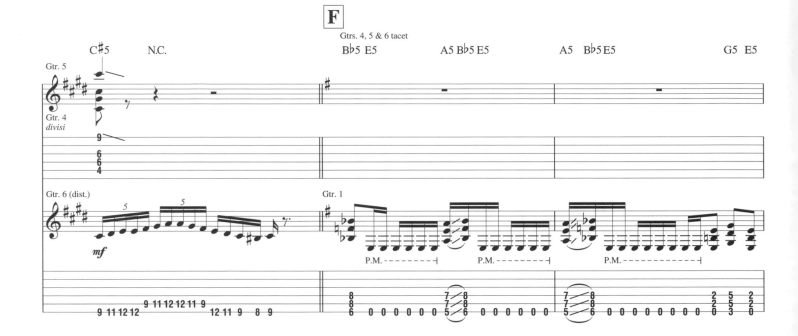

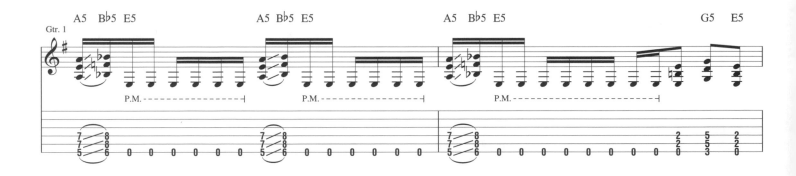

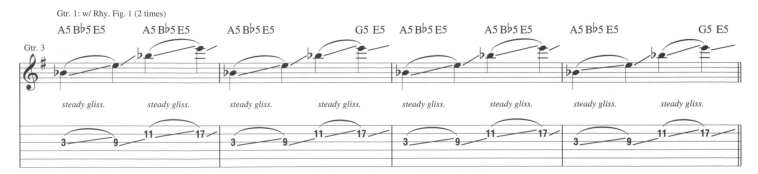

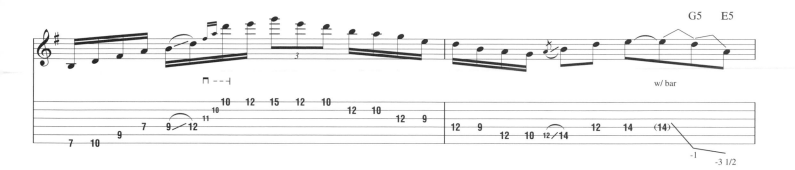

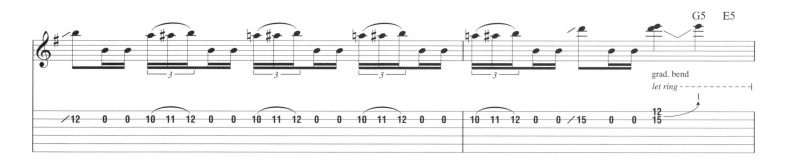

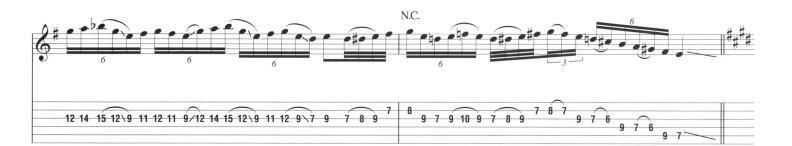

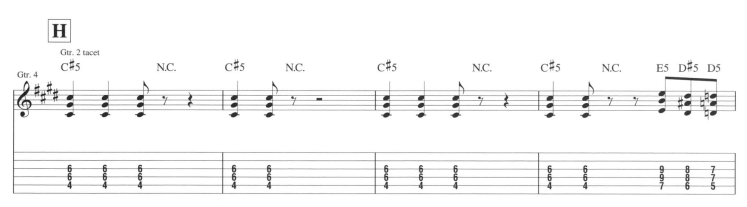

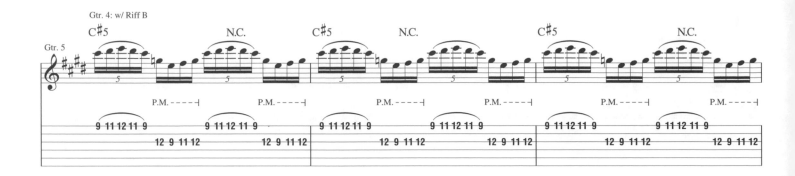

I

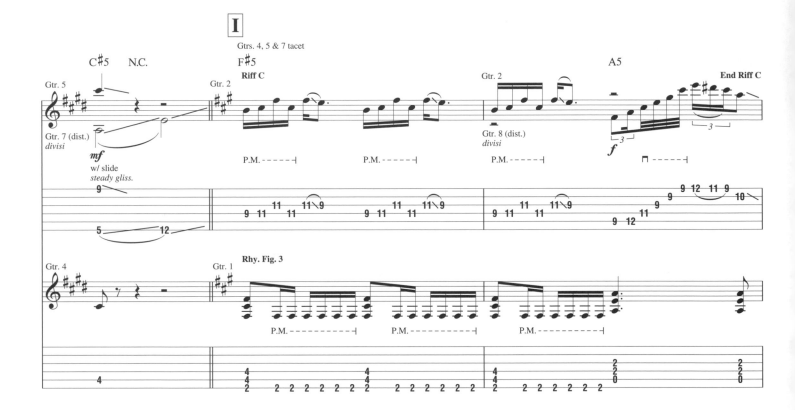

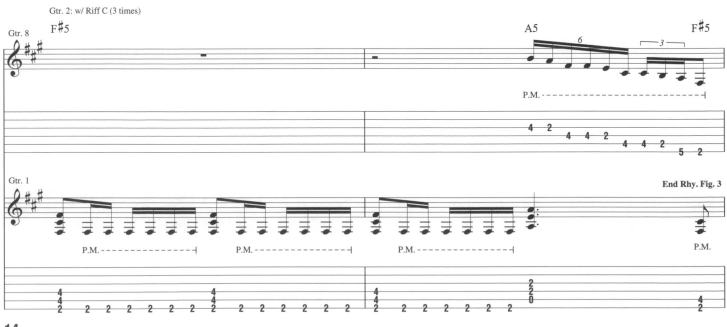

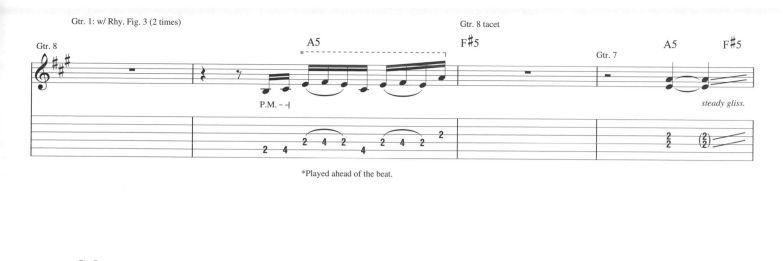

*Played ahead of the beat.

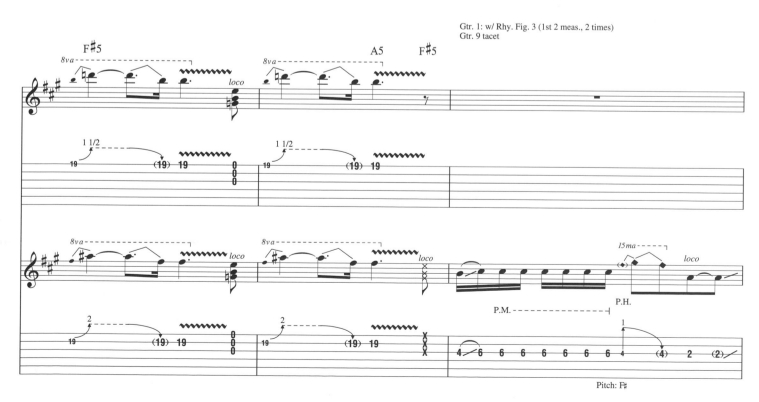

Pitch: F#

J

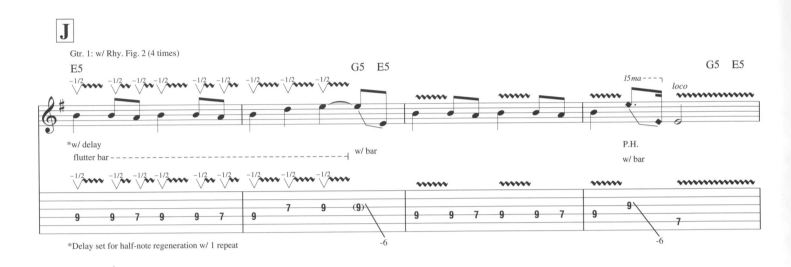

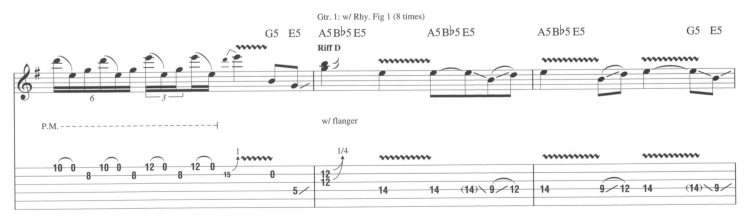

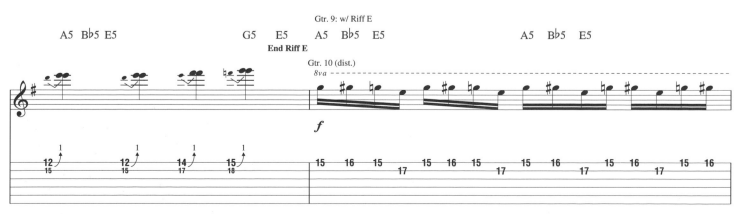

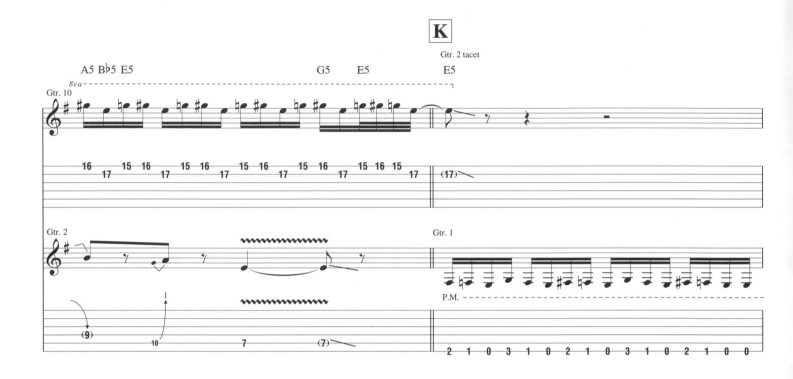

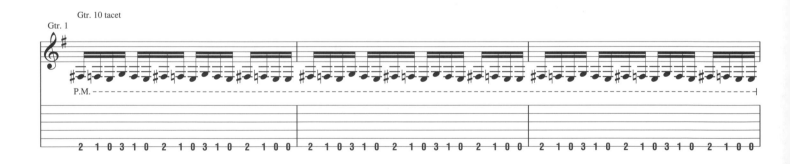

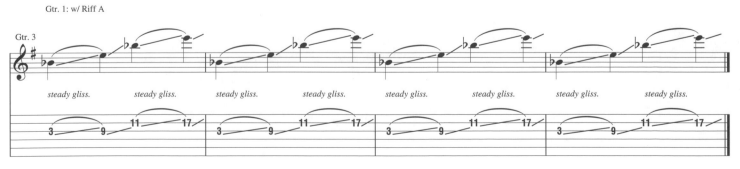

Feisty Cadavers

Music by John 5 and Kevin Savigar

Drop B tuning:
(low to high) B-A-D-G-B-E

A

Moderately fast ♩ = 129

*B5

Gtr. 1 (nylon-str. acous.)

mf

*Chord symbols reflect basic harmony.

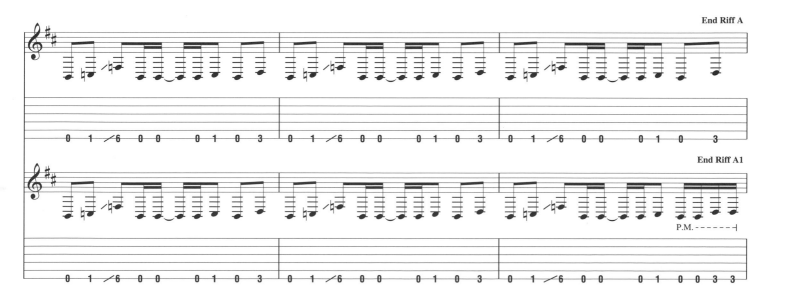

Gtrs. 2 & 3: w/ Riffs A & A1

Riff B

*Gtr. 4   *8va*- -

*Sequencer arr. for gtr.

B

Gtr. 4 tacet

B5

Gtr. 5 (elec.)

End Riff B

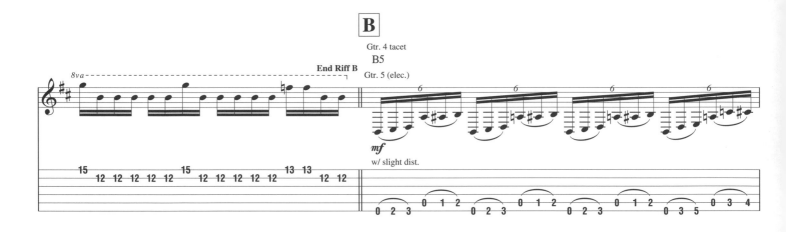

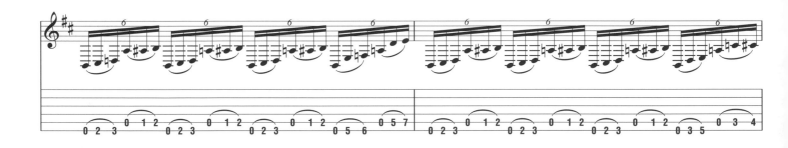

C

Gtr. 1: w/ Riff A

Gtr. 5 tacet

N.C.

B5

Gtr. 2

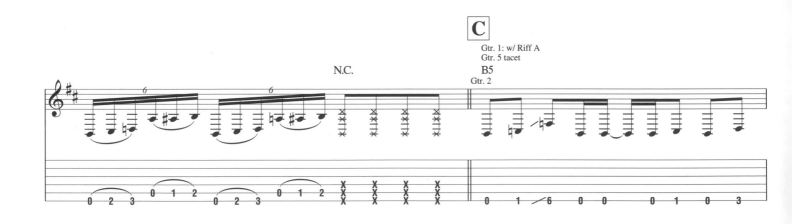

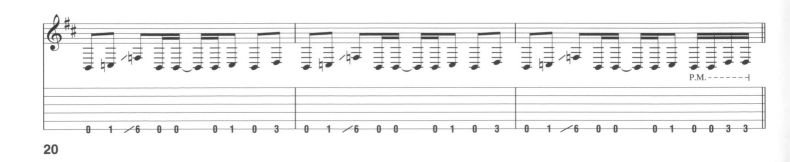

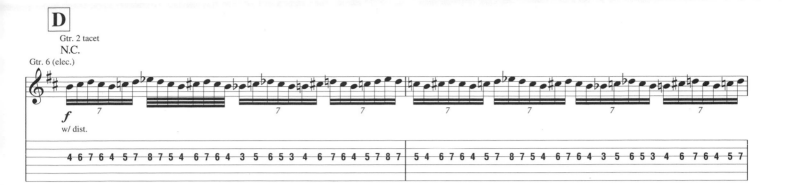

*Pick while sliding up.
Pitches are approximate.

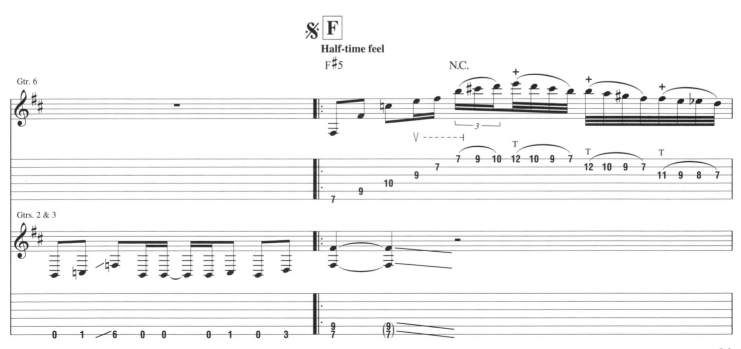

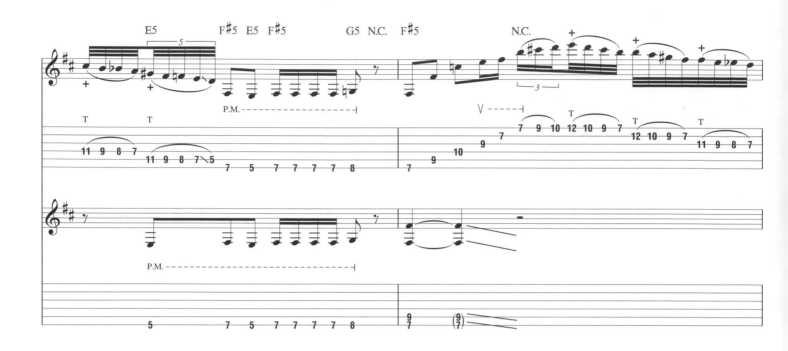

G

End half-time feel

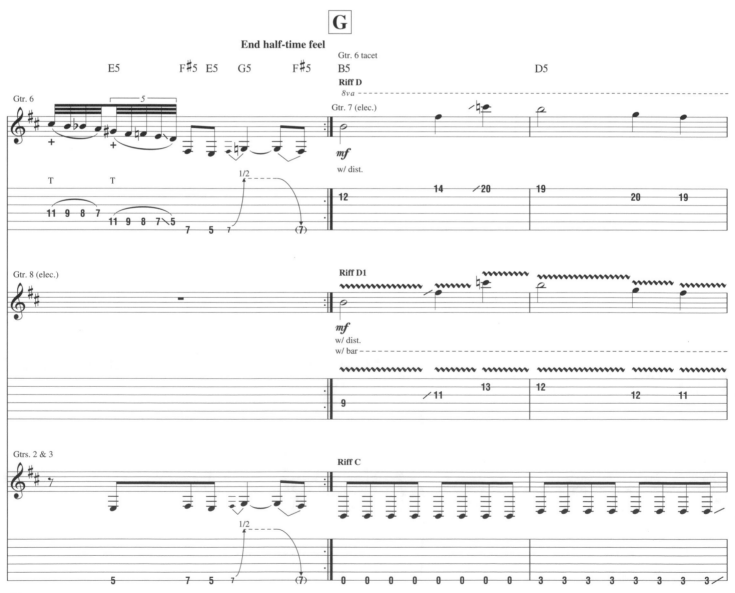

H

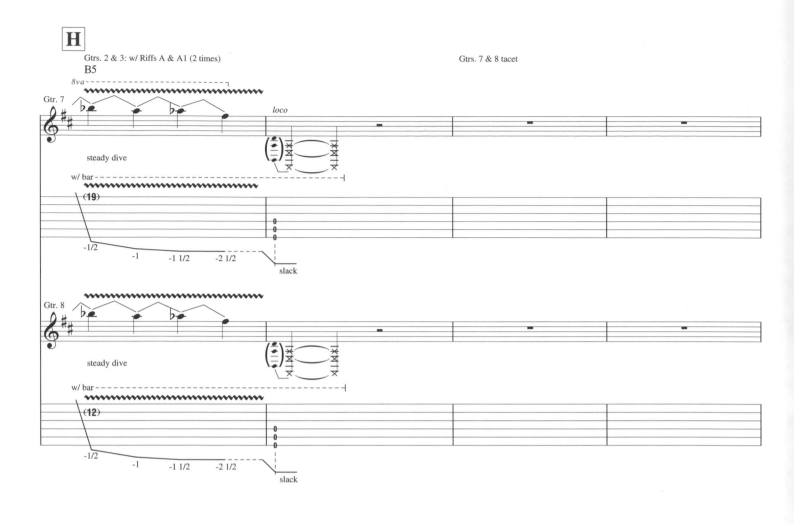

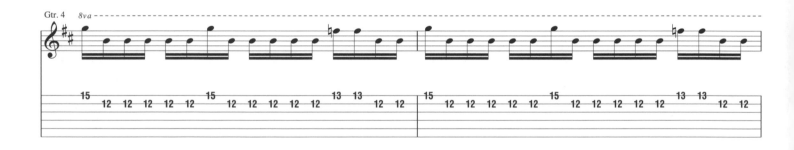

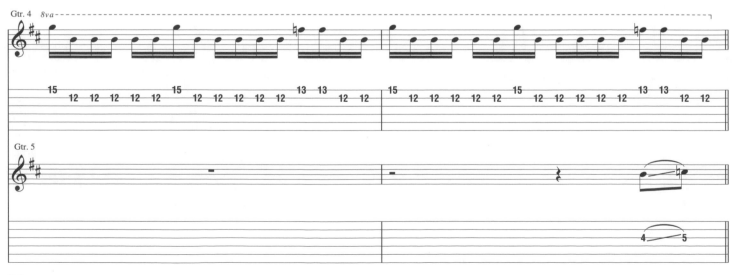

I

Gtr. 4 tacet

Gtr. 5   N.C.

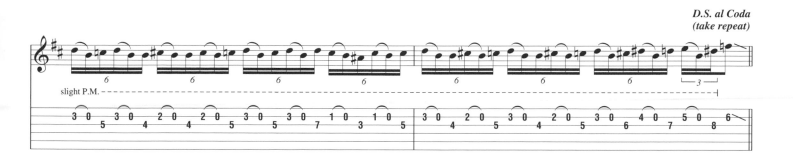

D.S. al Coda
(take repeat)

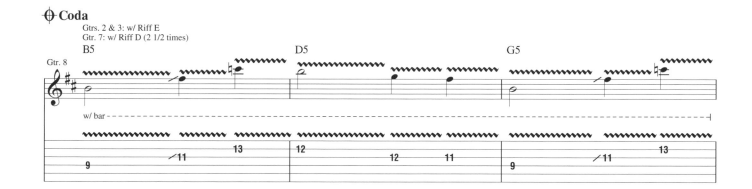

⊕ Coda

Gtrs. 2 & 3: w/ Riff E
Gtr. 7: w/ Riff D (2 1/2 times)

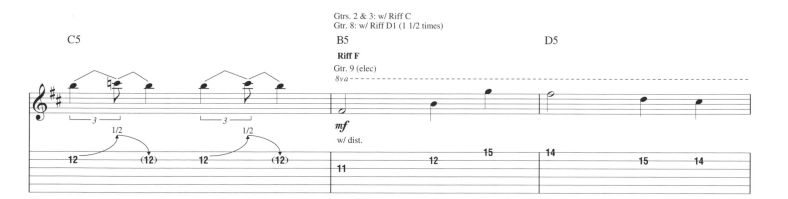

Gtrs. 2 & 3: w/ Riff C
Gtr. 8: w/ Riff D1 (1 1/2 times)

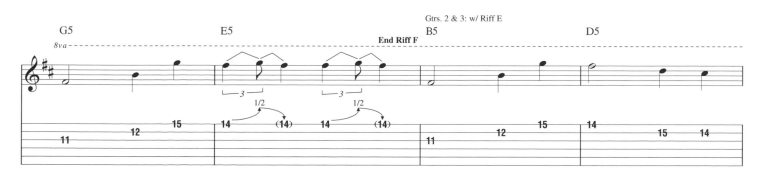

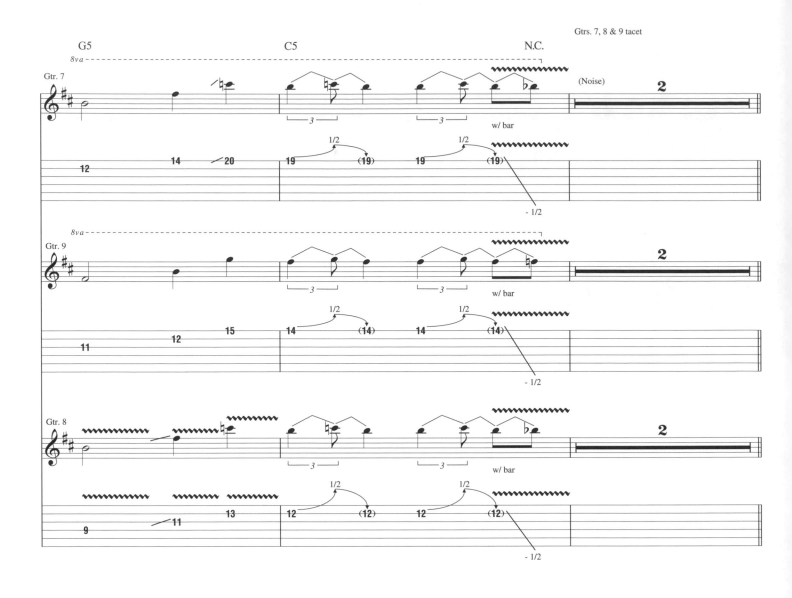

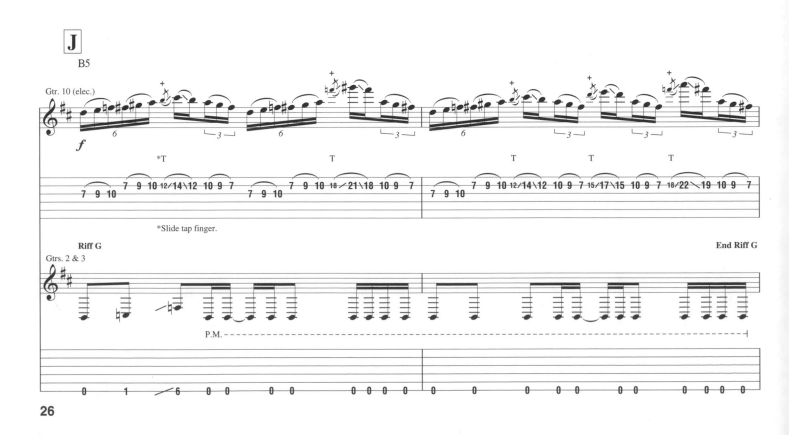

Gtr. 10

Gtrs. 2 & 3: w/ Riff G (5 times)

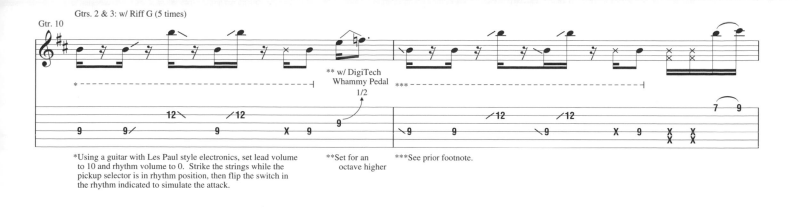

** w/ DigiTech
Whammy Pedal
1/2

***

*Using a guitar with Les Paul style electronics, set lead volume to 10 and rhythm volume to 0. Strike the strings while the pickup selector is in rhythm position, then flip the switch in the rhythm indicated to simulate the attack.

**Set for an octave higher

***See prior footnote.

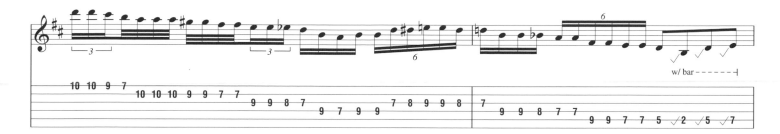

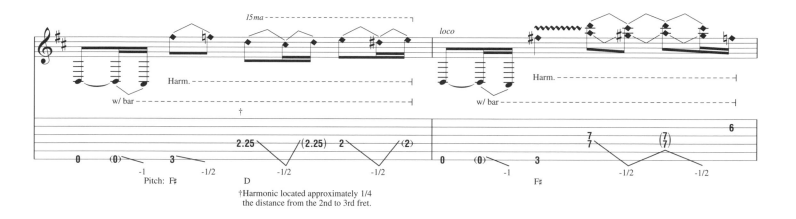

Pitch: F♯   D   F♯

†Harmonic located approximately 1/4 the distance from the 2nd to 3rd fret.

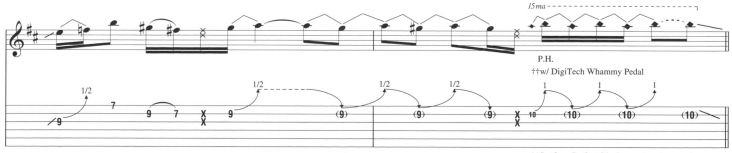

P.H.

††w/ DigiTech Whammy Pedal

††Set for a Perfect 5th above when depressed.

K

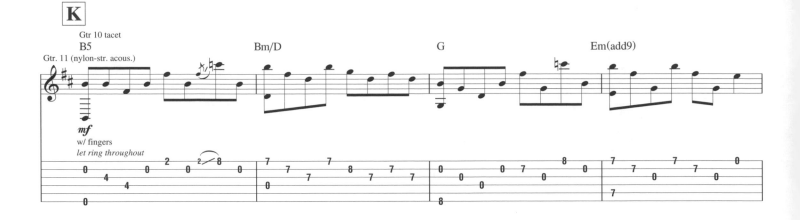

L

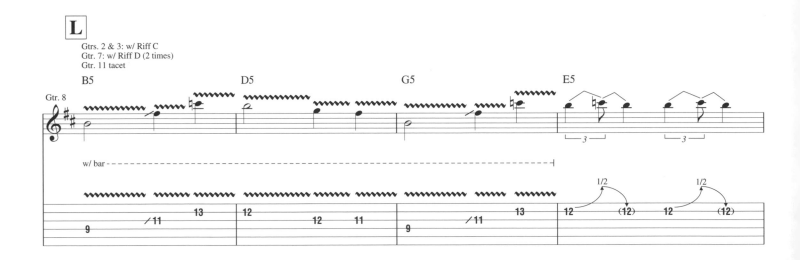

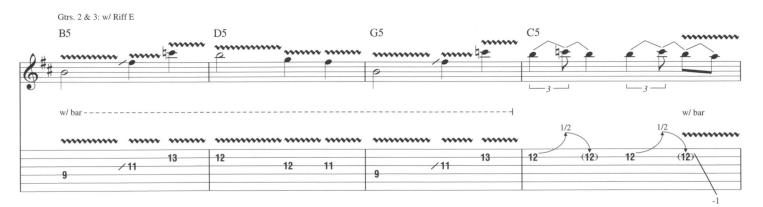

Gtrs. 2 & 3: w/ Riff C
Gtr. 8: tacet

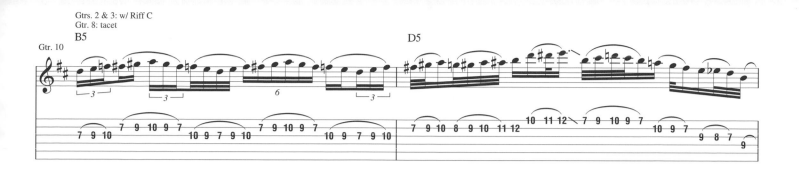

Gtrs. 2 & 3: w/ Riff E
Gtr. 7: w/ Riff D
Gtr. 9: w/ Riff F
Gtr. 10 tacet

Gtrs. 2 & 3: w/ Riff C
Gtr. 4: w/ Riff B (2 times)
Gtr. 7: w/ Riff D (2 times)
Gtr. 9: w/ Riff F (2 times)

Repeat and fade

Gtrs. 2 & 3: w/ Riff E

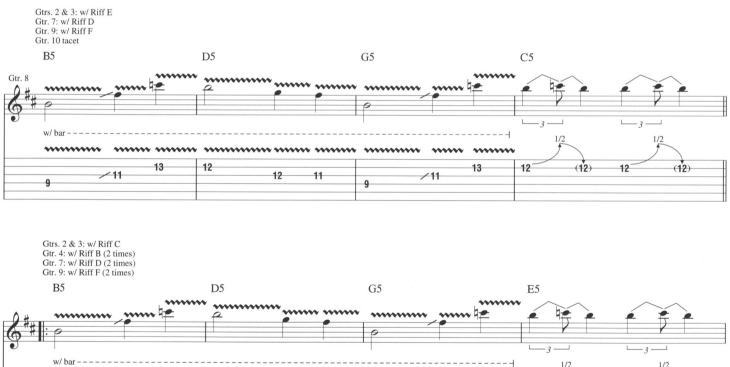

Pulling Strings

Music by John 5 and Kevin Savigar

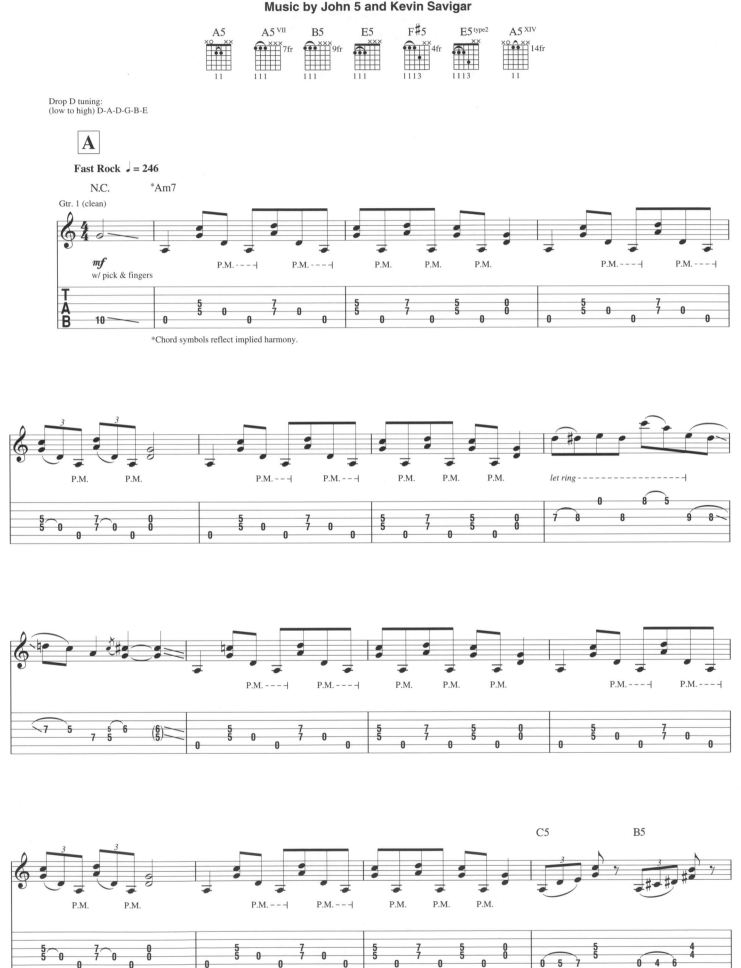

Drop D tuning:
(low to high) D-A-D-G-B-E

Fast Rock ♩ = 246

N.C.   *Am7

Gtr. 1 (clean)

mf
w/ pick & fingers

*Chord symbols reflect implied harmony.

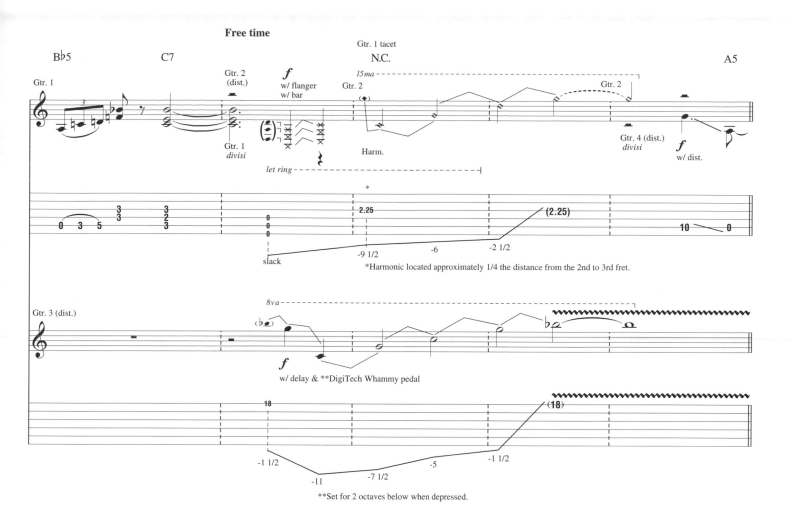

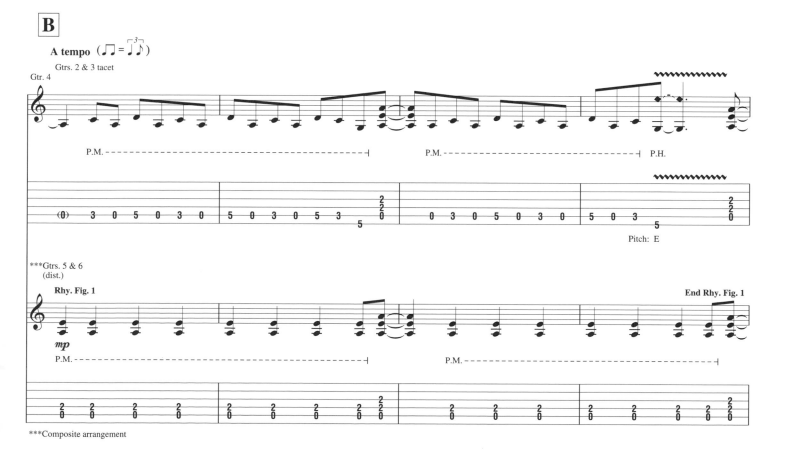

***Composite arrangement

*Slide tap finger.

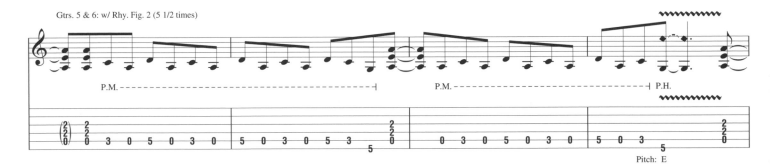

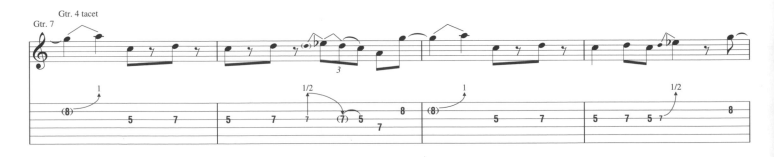

D

Gtrs. 5 & 6: w/ Rhy. Fig. 2 (3 1/2 times)
Gtr. 8 tacet

*Produce harmonic by tapping string an octave above fretted note.

Pitch: E

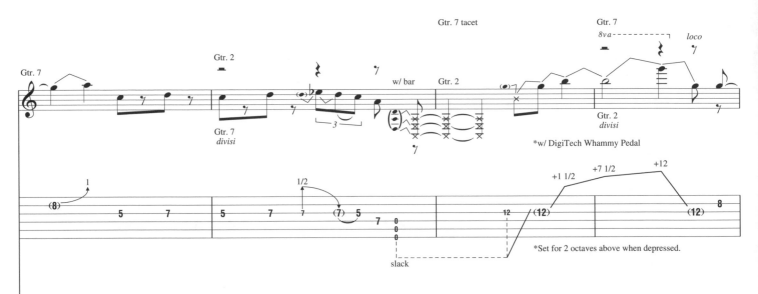

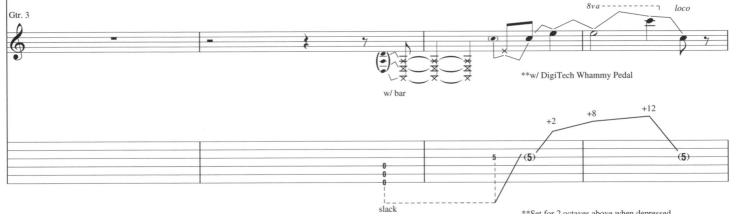

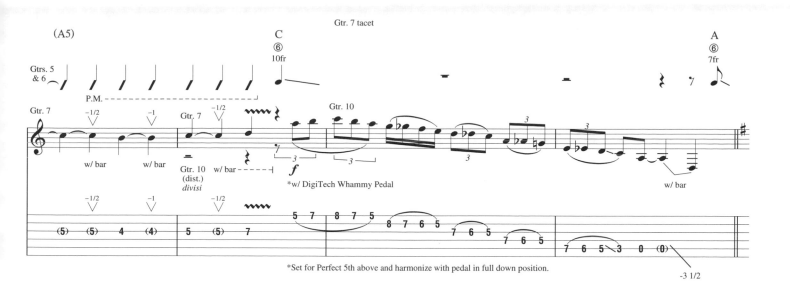

*w/ DigiTech Whammy Pedal

*Set for Perfect 5th above and harmonize with pedal in full down position.

E

Gtrs. 5 & 6: w/ Rhy. Fig. 3
Gtr. 10 tacet

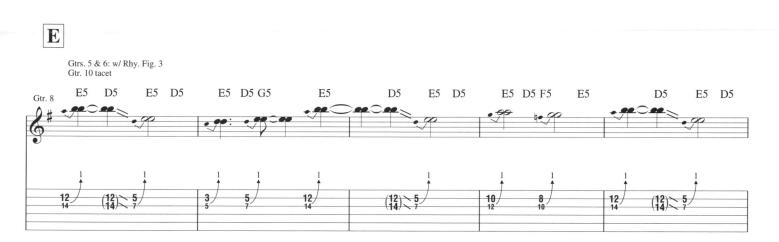

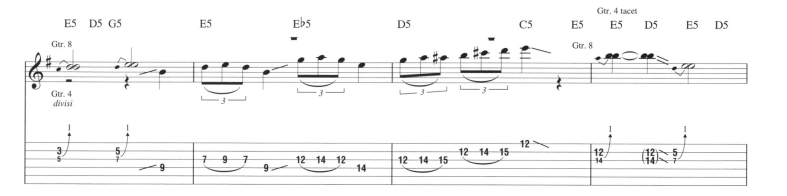

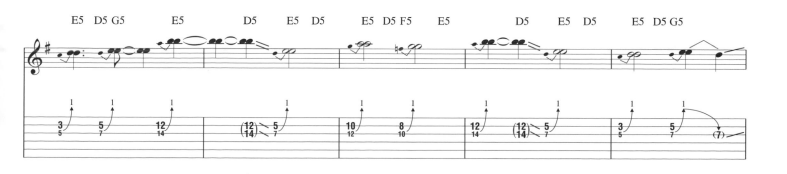

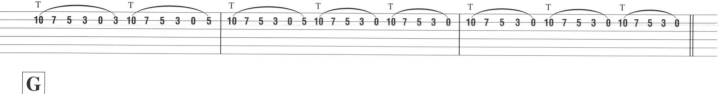

G

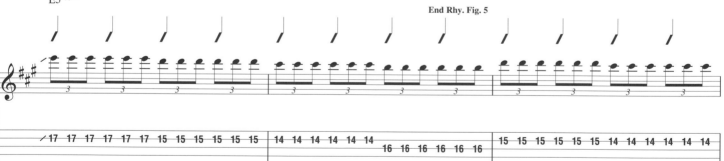

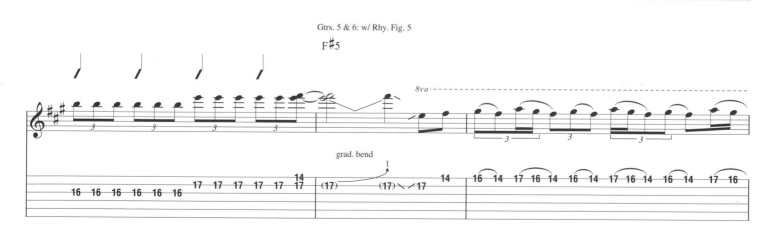

Free time

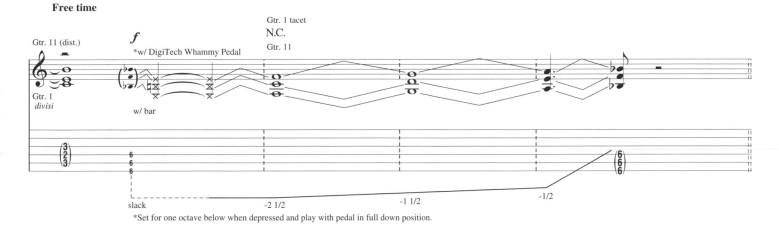

*Set for one octave below when depressed and play with pedal in full down position.

I

A tempo $\left(\; \prod = \overline{}^{\;3\;} \;\right)$

Gtrs. 5 & 6: w/ Rhy. Fig. 1
Gtr. 11 tacet

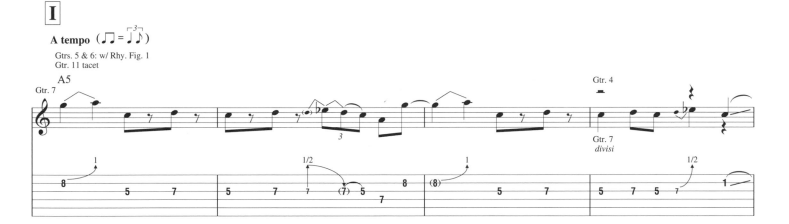

Gtrs. 5 & 6: w/ Rhy. Fig. 2 (3 times)
Gtr. 7 tacet

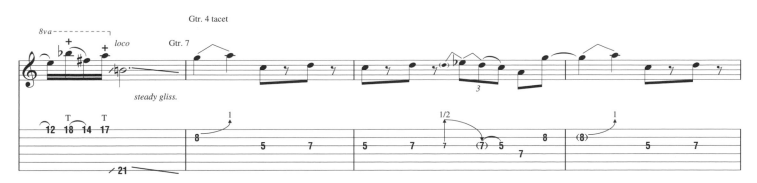

*Played as even eighth notes.

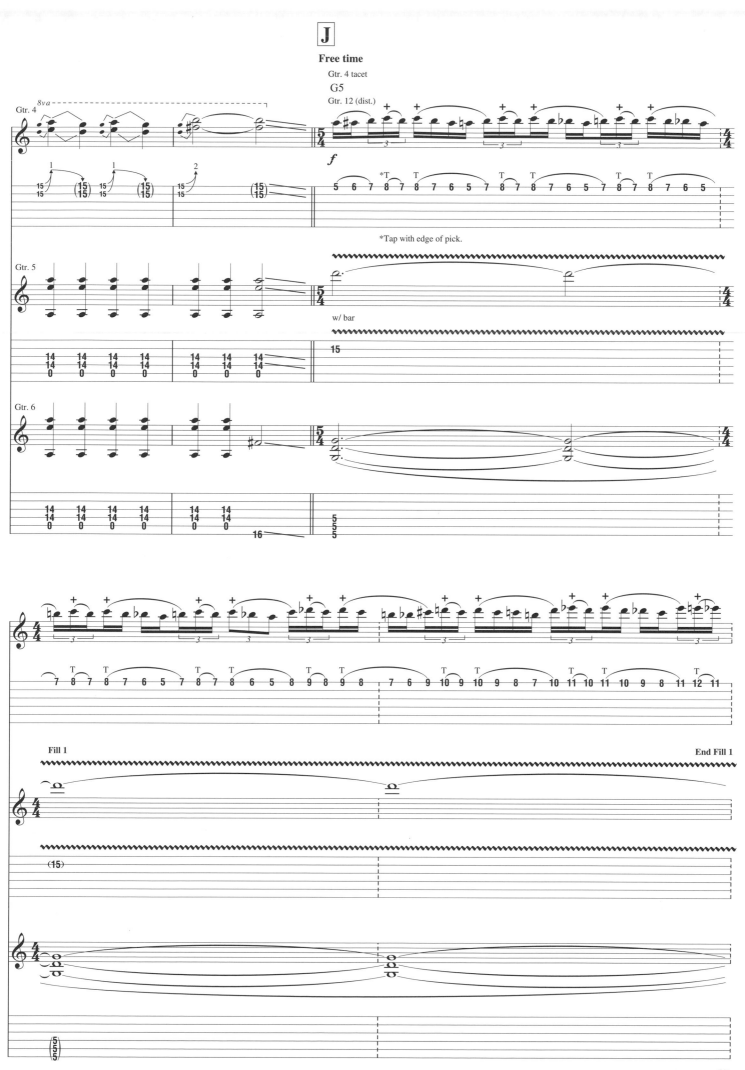

Gtr. 5: w/ Fill 1 (till tape cut)

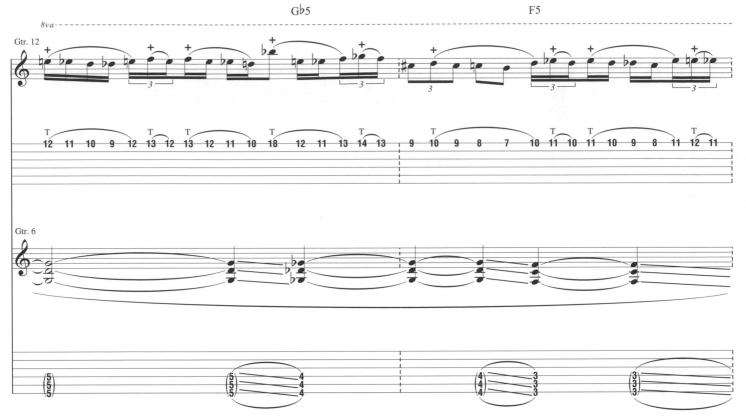

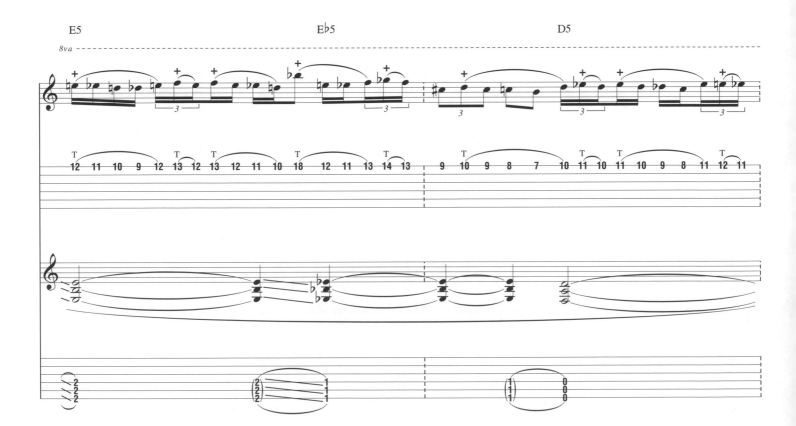

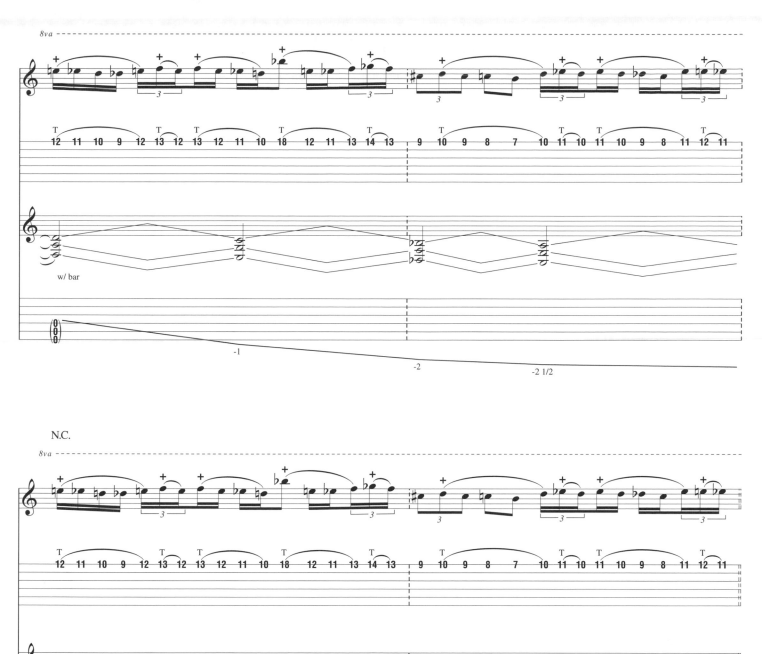

N.C.

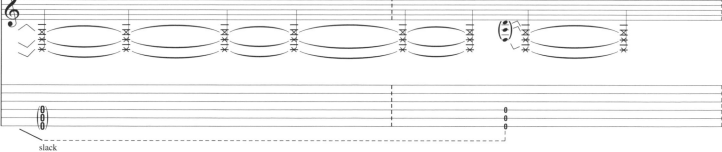

slack

Gtr. 6 tacet

N.C.

Play 8 times
(simulated tape cut)

Gtr. 12

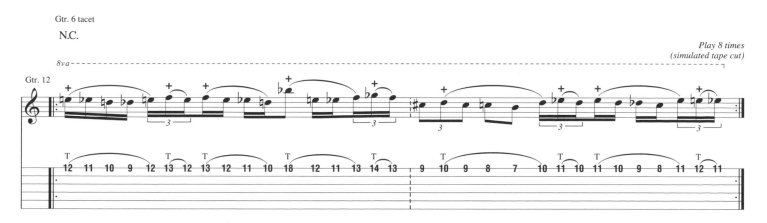

Sugarfoot Rag

Words and Music by Hank Garland and Vaughn Horton

*Chord symbols reflect basic harmony.

**Microphonic fdbk., not caused by string vibration.

***T = Thumb on 6th string

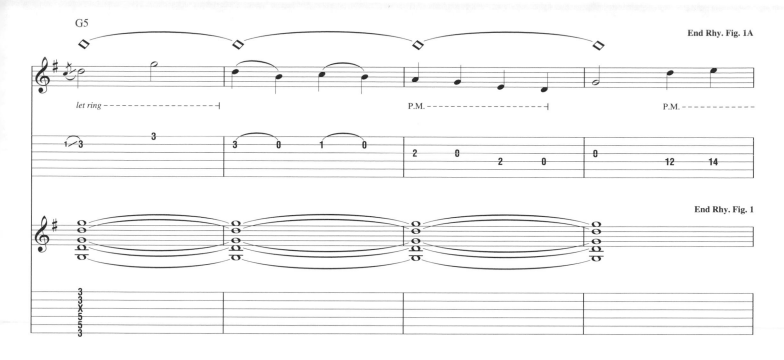

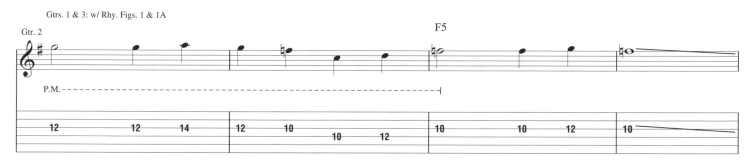

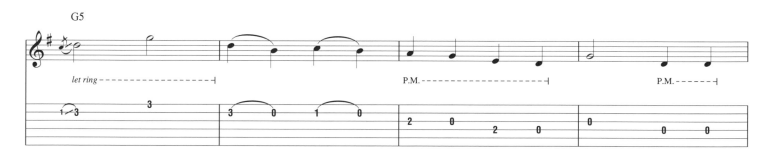

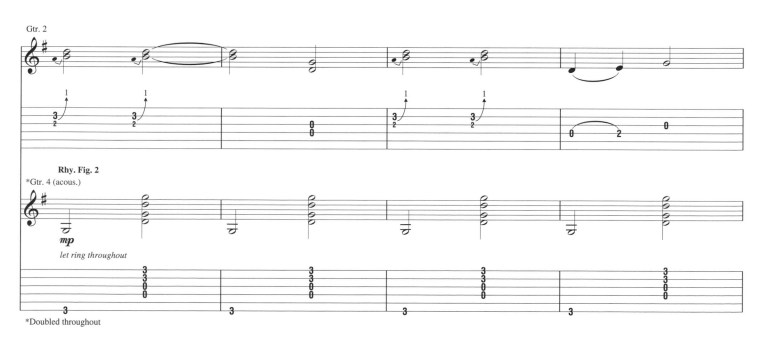

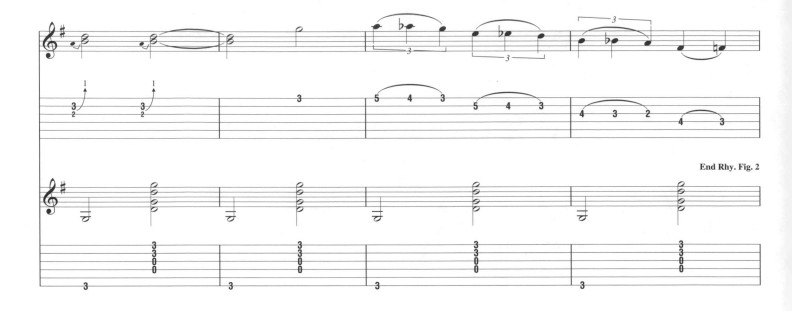

End Rhy. Fig. 2

Gtr. 4: w/ Rhy. Fig. 2

Gtr. 2

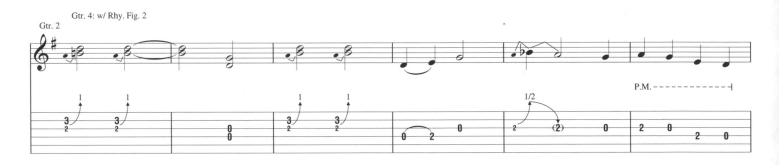

C

Gtrs. 1 & 3: w/ Rhy. Figs. 1 & 1A (2 times)
Gtr. 2 tacet

G5   F5

Gtr. 5
(elec.)

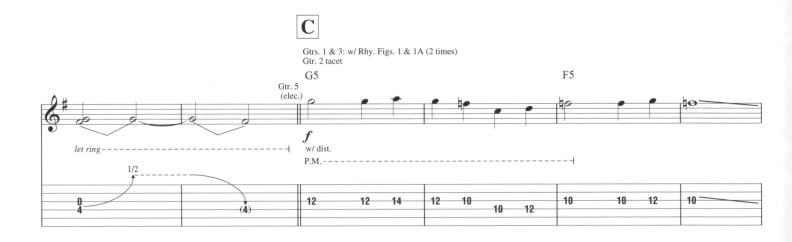

G5

Voc. Fig. 1   **End Voc. Fig. 1**

(Ah.)

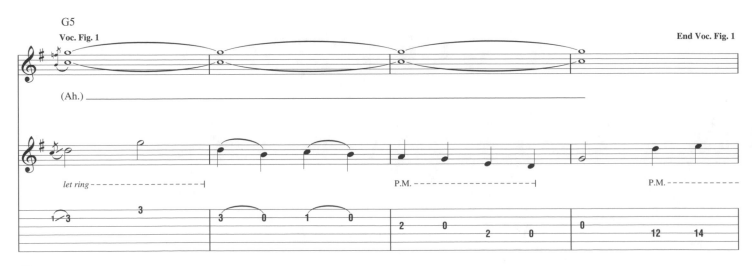

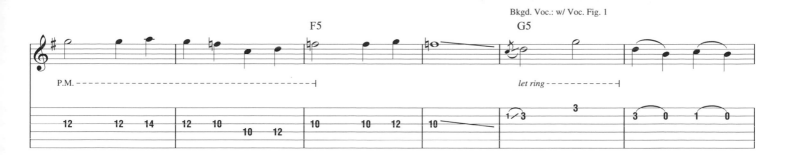

D

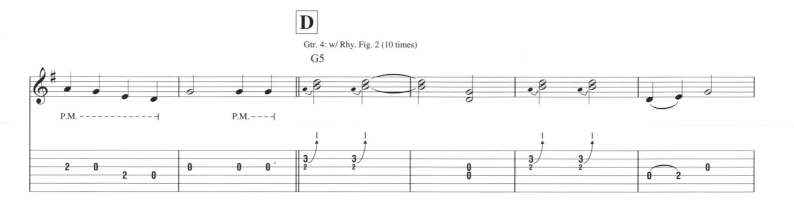

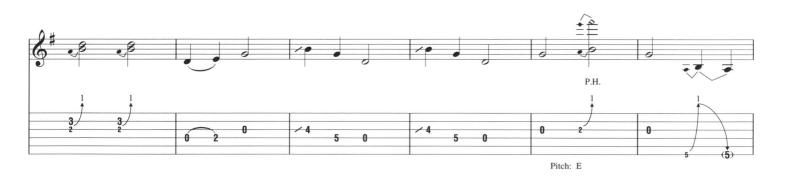

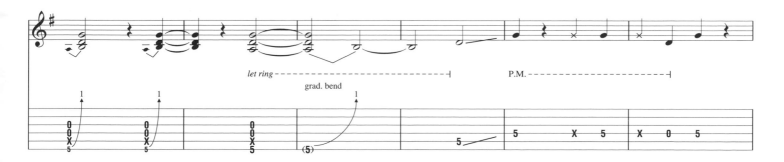

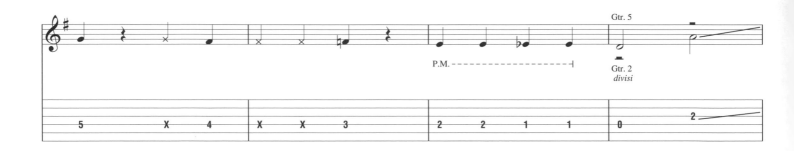

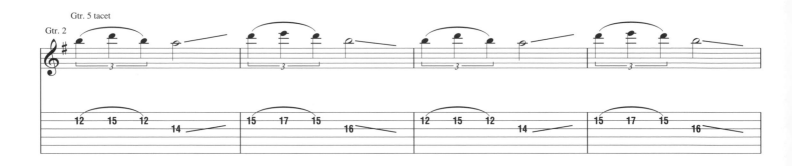

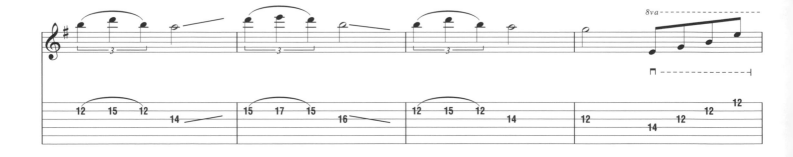

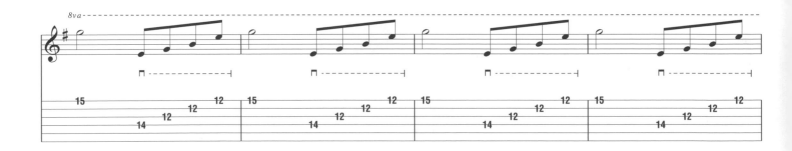

50

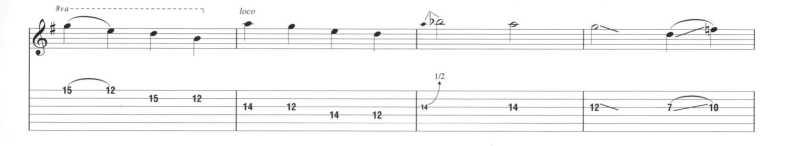

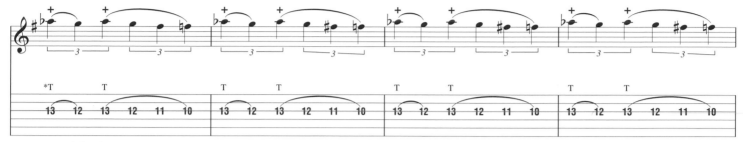

*Tap w/ edge of pick (next 8 meas.).

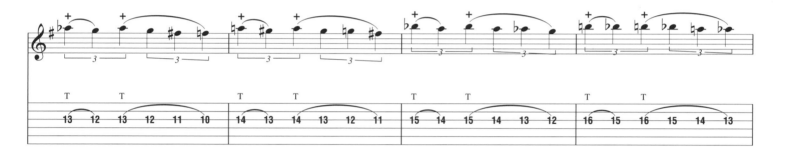

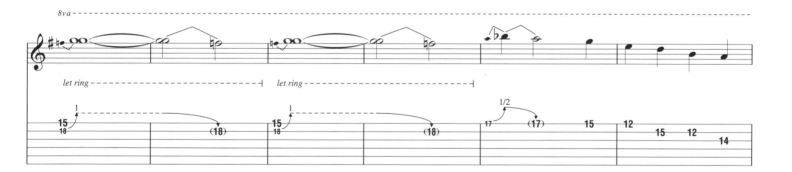

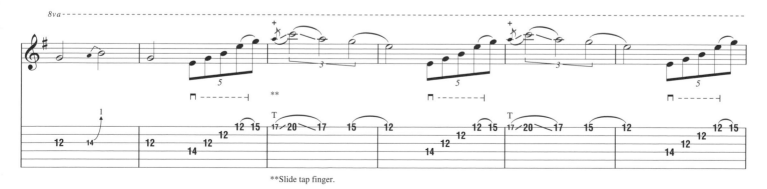

**Slide tap finger.

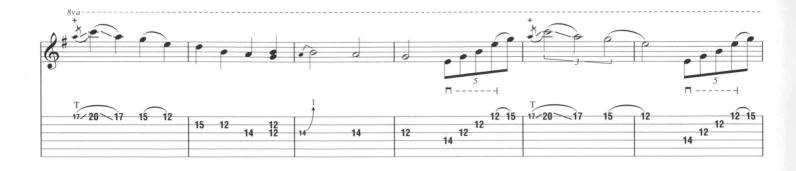

E

Gtrs. 1 & 3: w/ Rhy. Figs. 1 & 1A (1st 4 meas.)
Gtr. 2 tacet

Gtr. 4: w/ Rhy. Fig. 2 (last 4 meas.)

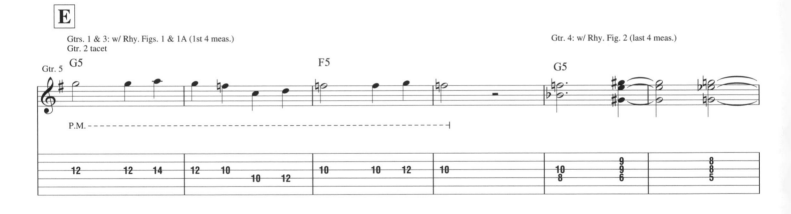

Gtrs. 1 & 3: w/ Rhy. Figs. 1 & 1A (1st 4 meas.)

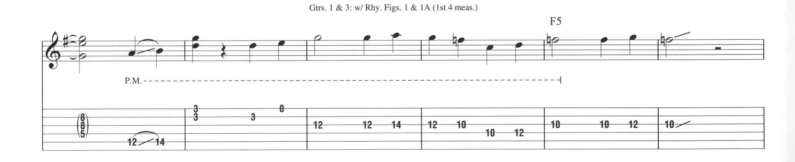

Gtr. 4: w/ Rhy. Fig. 2 (last 4 meas.)

Gtr. 4: w/ Rhy. Fig. 2 (10 times)
Gtr. 5 tacet

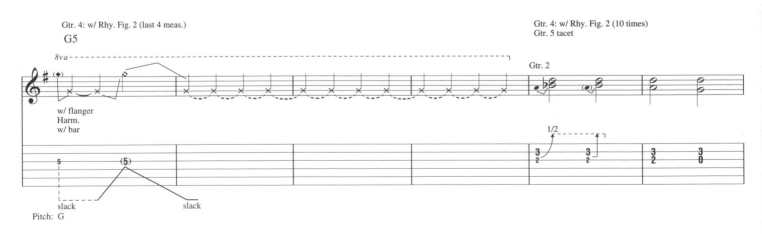

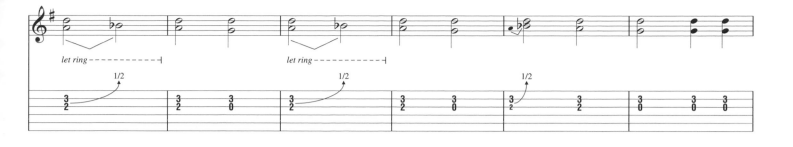

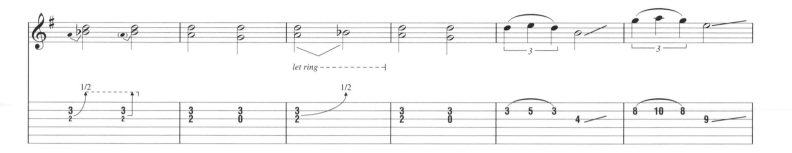

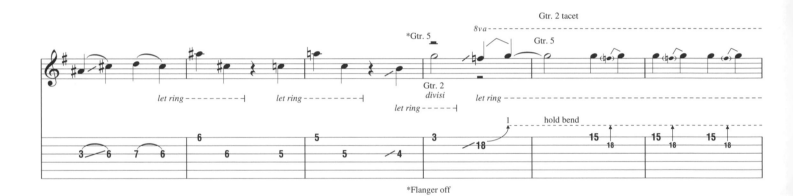

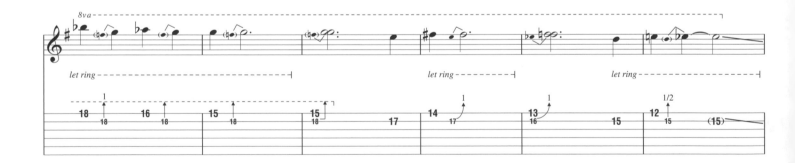

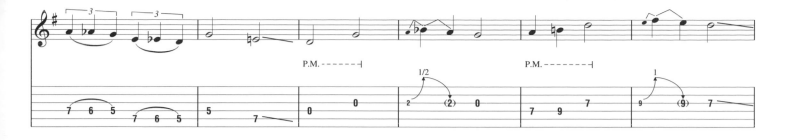

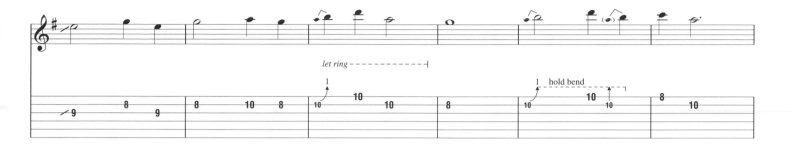

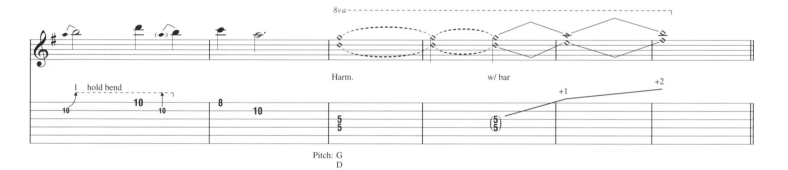

Pitch: G
        D

F

Gtrs. 1 & 3: w/ Rhy. Figs. 1 & 1A (2 times)
Gtr. 5 tacet

Bkgd. Voc.: w/ Voc. Fig. 1
Gtr. 4: w/ Rhy. Fig. 2 (last 4 meas.)

Gtr. 2 G5   F5   G5

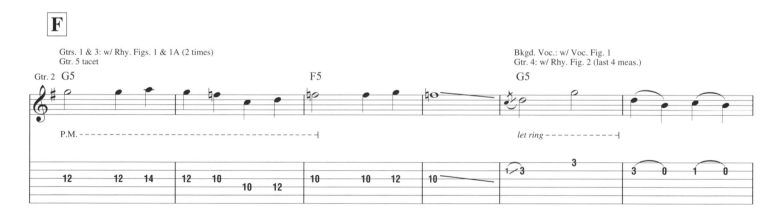

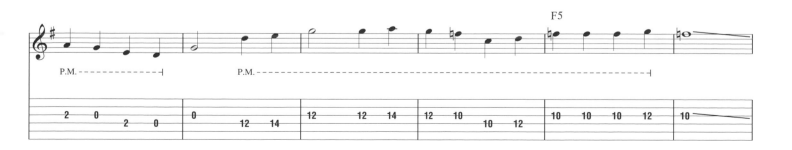

Bkgd. Voc.: w/ Voc. Fig. 1
Gtr. 4: w/ Rhy. Fig. 2 (last 4 meas.)

Gtr. 4: w/ Rhy. Fig. 2 (8 times)

*steady gliss.

*Pluck in eighth-note rhythm while sliding up fretboard. Pitches are approximate.

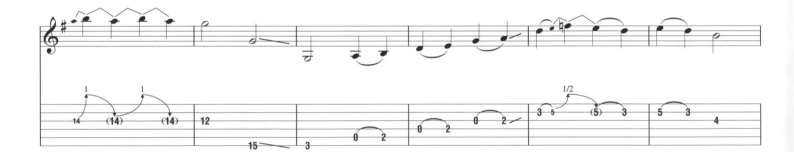

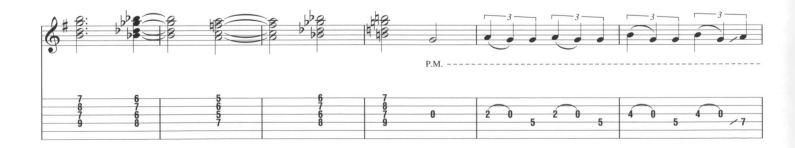

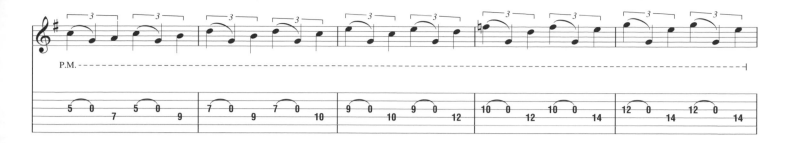

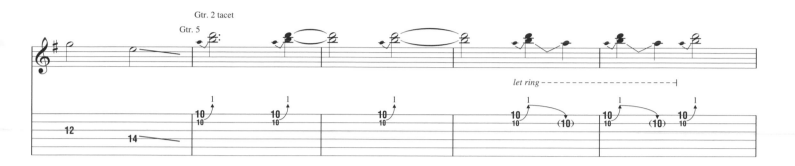

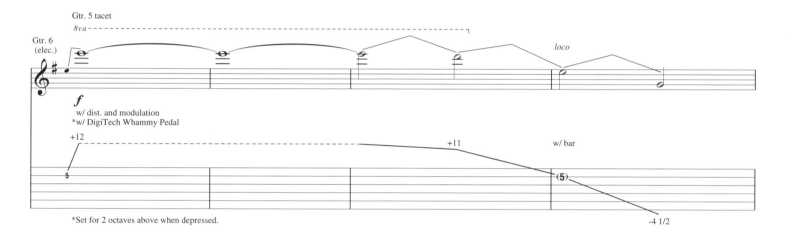

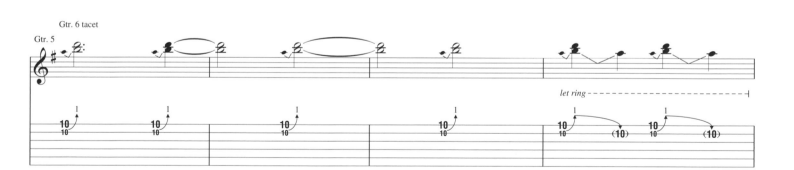

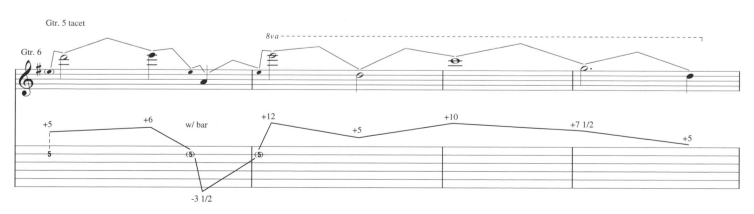

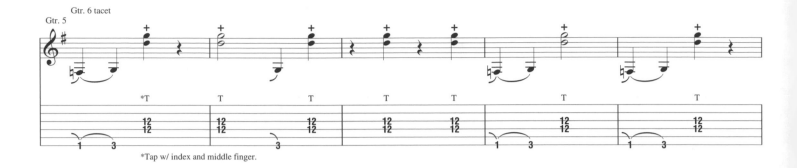

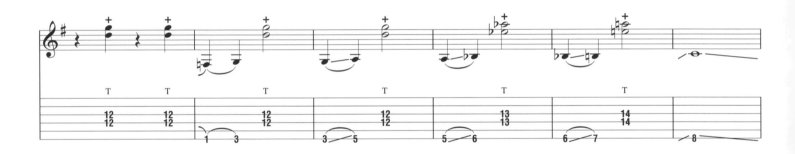

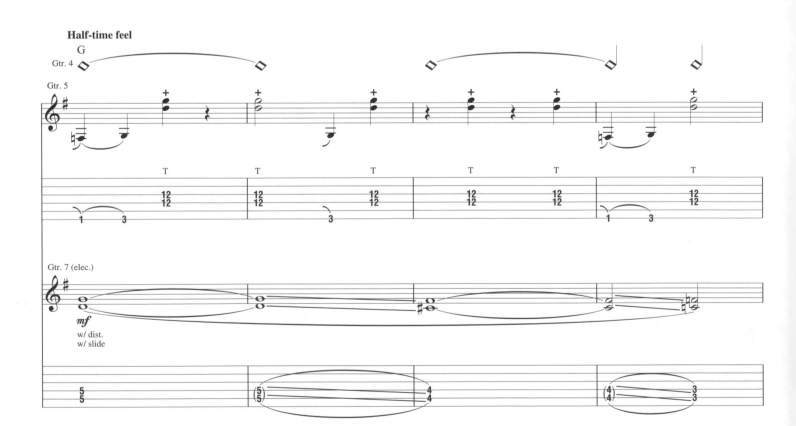

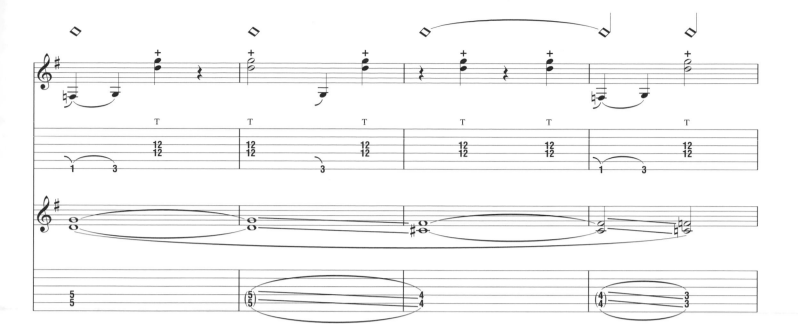

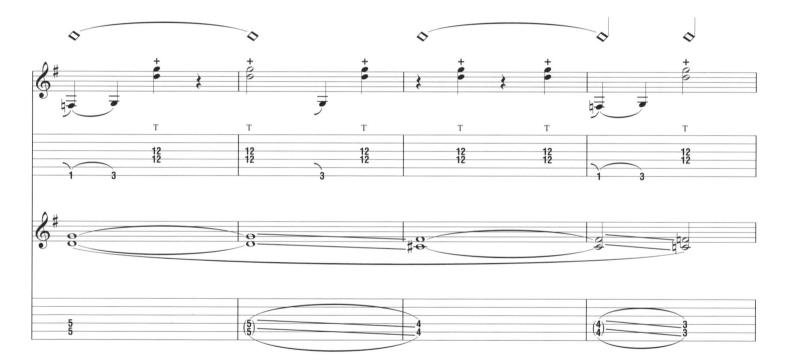

End half-time feel

Gtrs. 4 & 5 tacet

| G5 | F#5 | F5 | E5 | Eb5 |

Gtr. 7

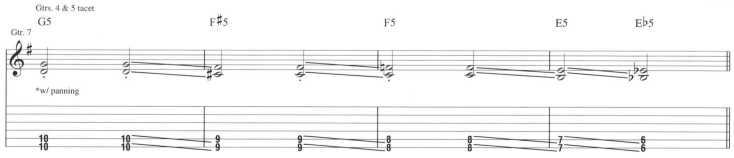

*w/ panning

*Slide down while oscillating between the left and right channels.

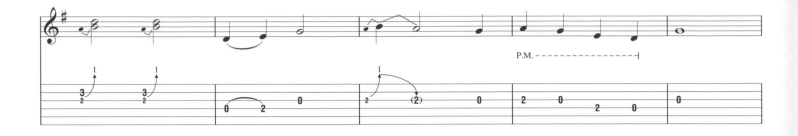

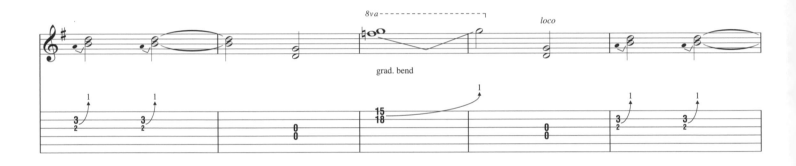

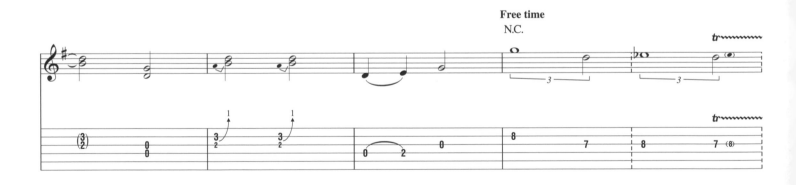

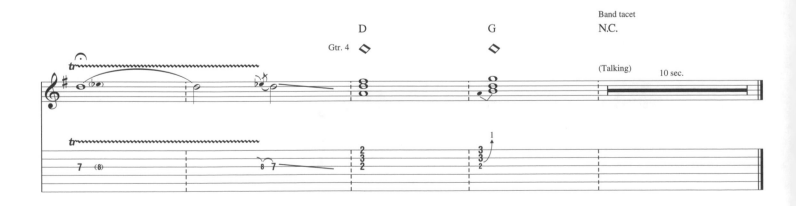

Dead Man's Dream

Music by John 5 and Kevin Savigar

Tune down 1/2 step:
(low to high) Eb-Ab-Db-Gb-Bb-Eb

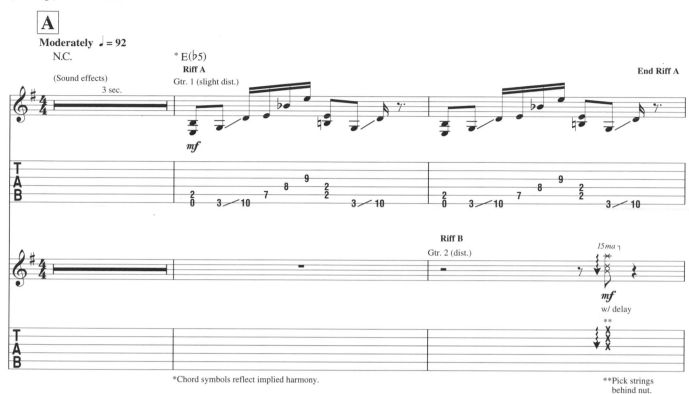

*Chord symbols reflect implied harmony.

**Pick strings behind nut.

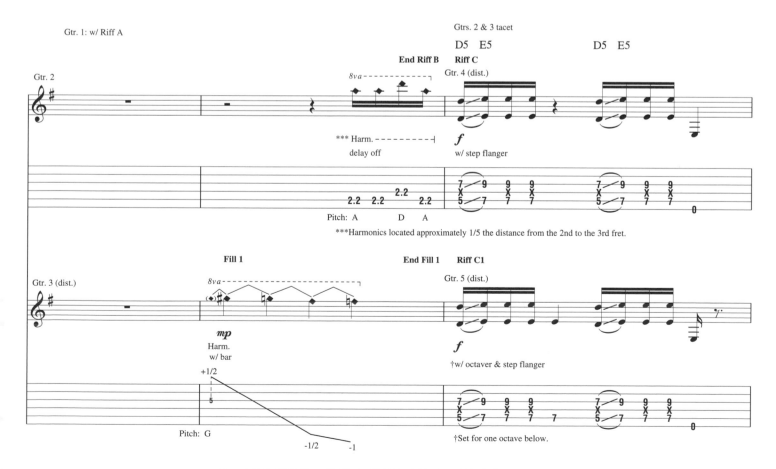

***Harmonics located approximately 1/5 the distance from the 2nd to the 3rd fret.

†Set for one octave below.

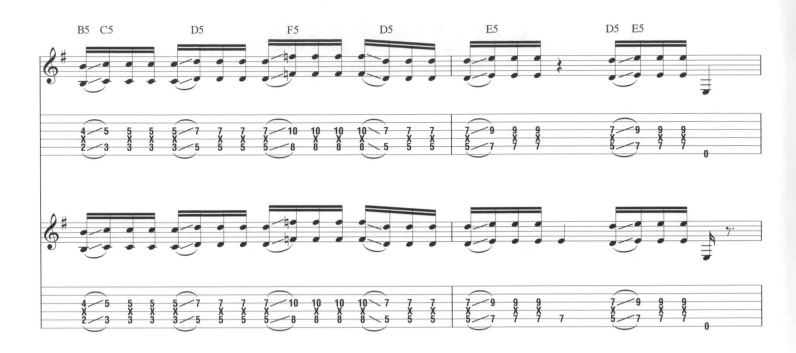

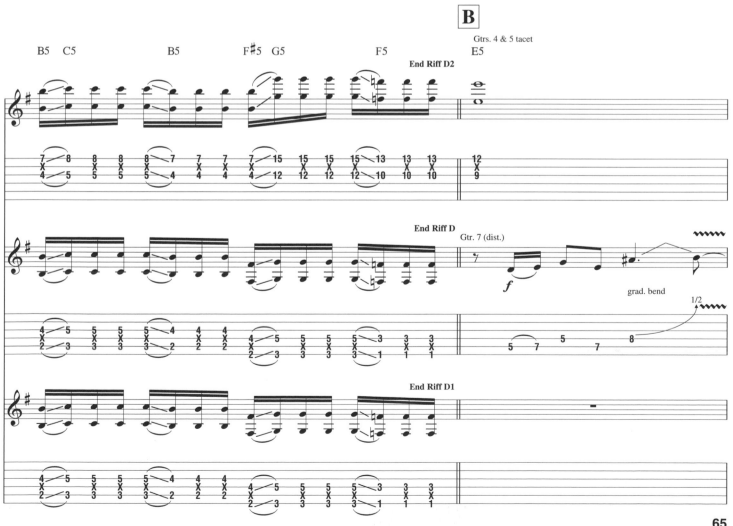

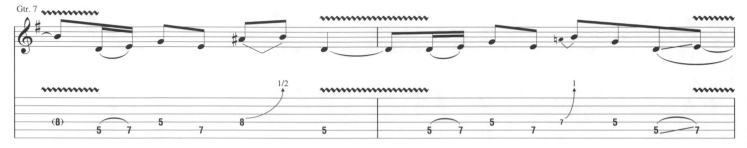

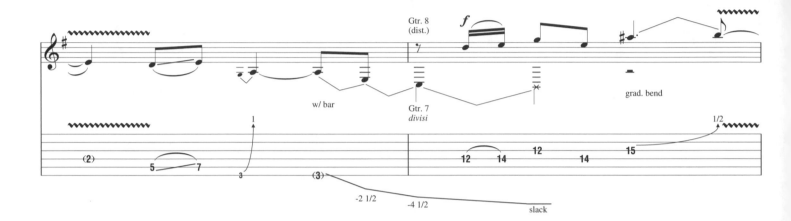

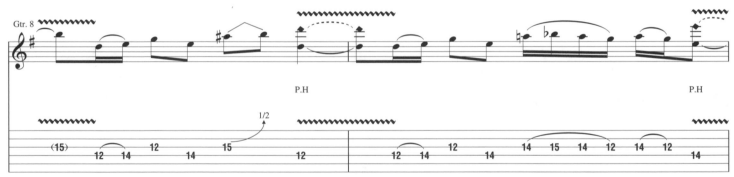

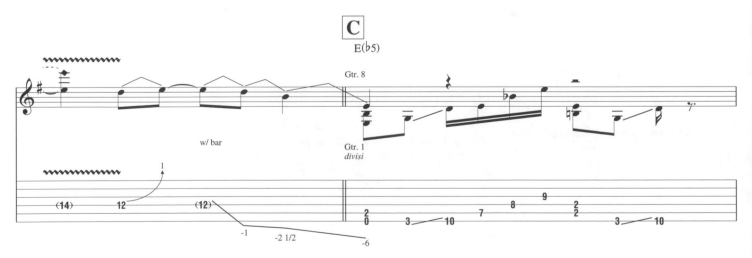

Gtr. 1 tacet

D5 E5   D5   E5   B5   C5   D5   F5   D5

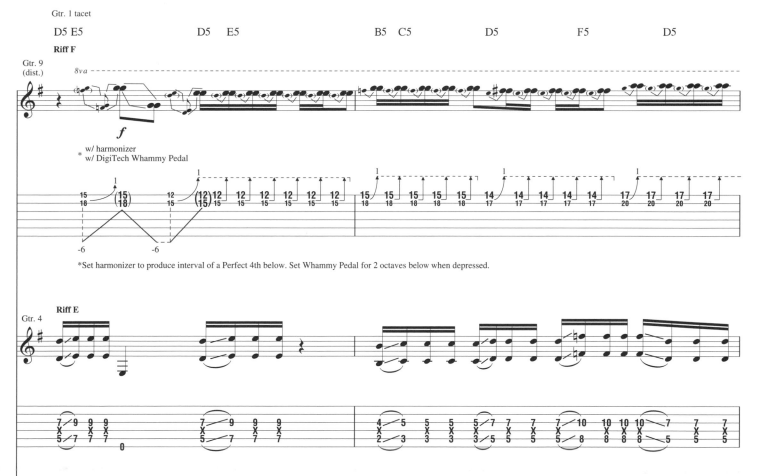

*Set harmonizer to produce interval of a Perfect 4th below. Set Whammy Pedal for 2 octaves below when depressed.

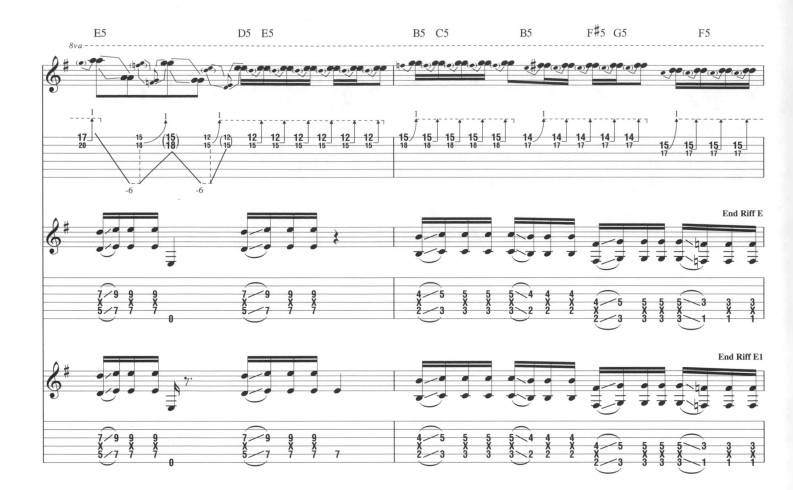

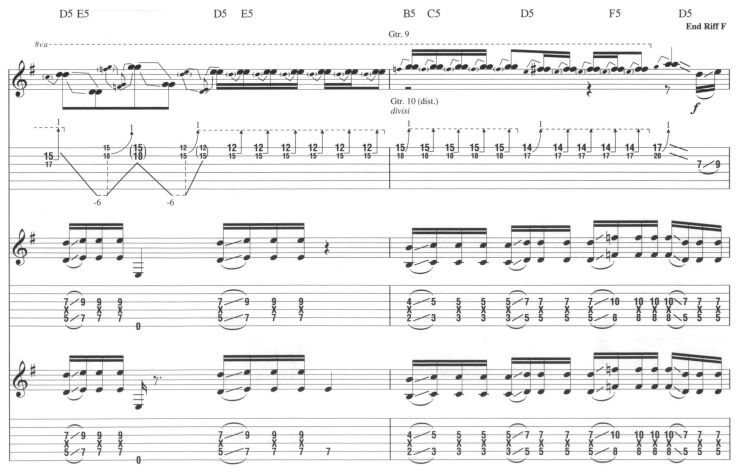

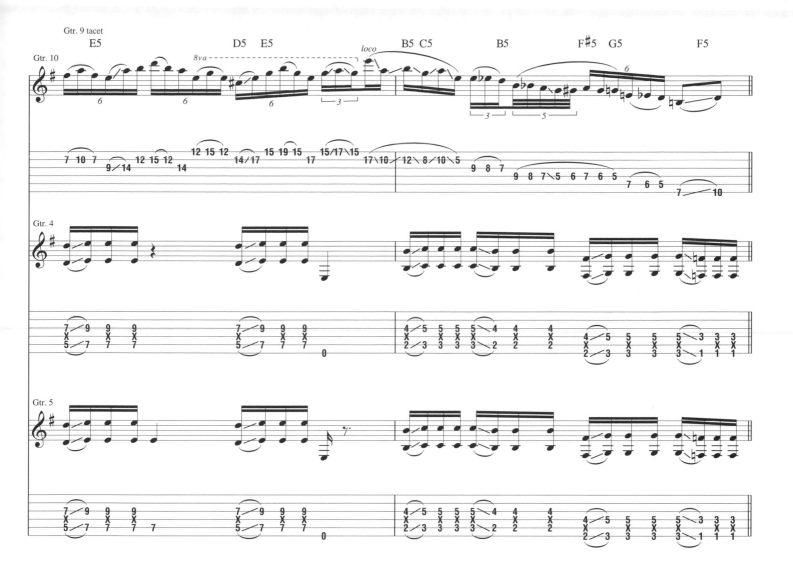

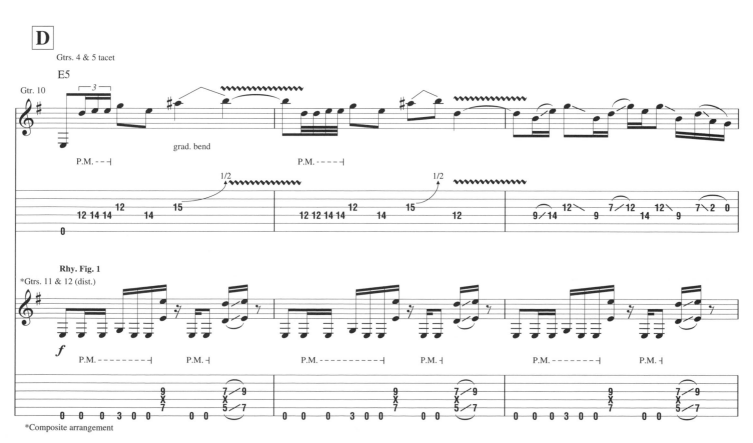

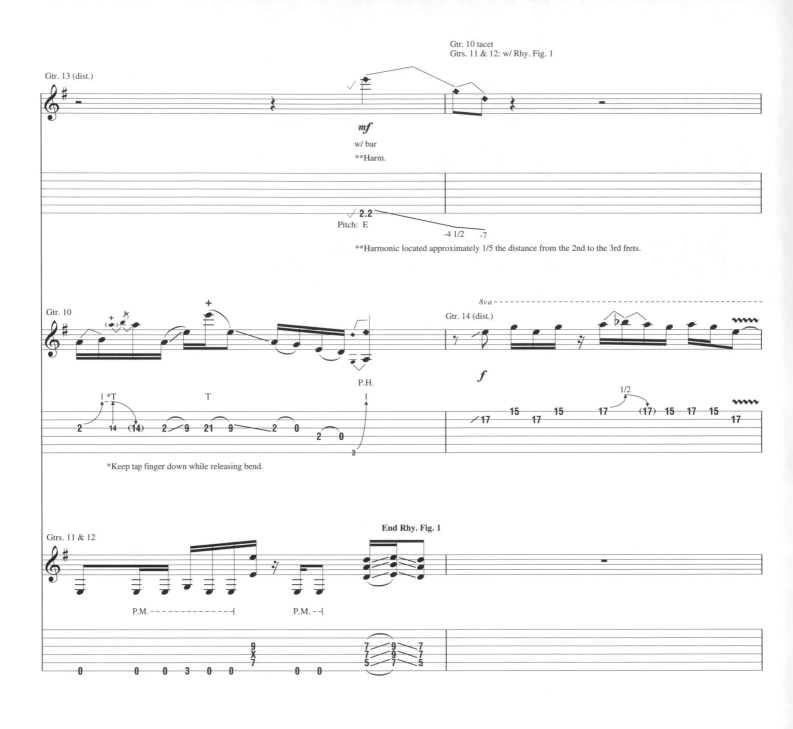

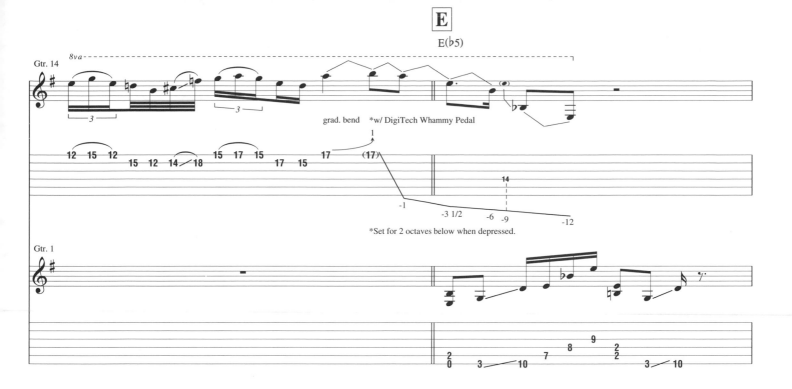

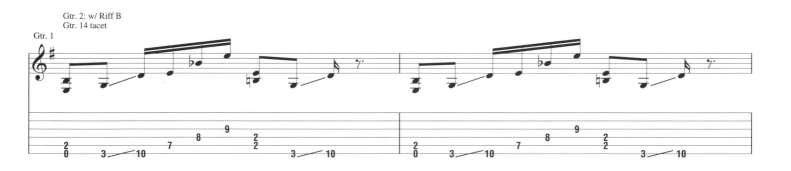

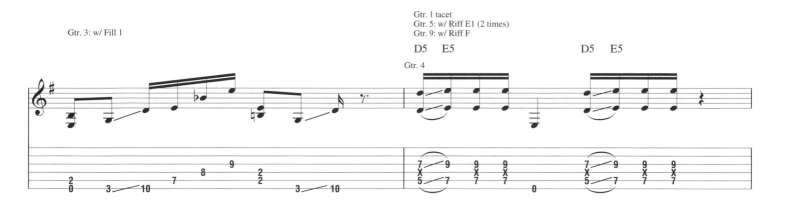

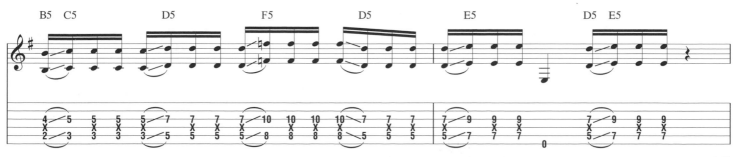

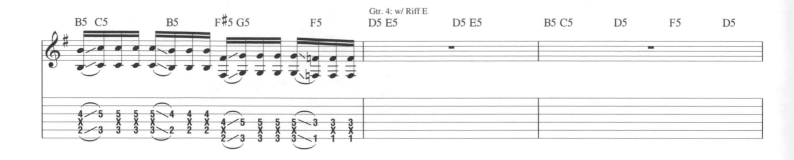

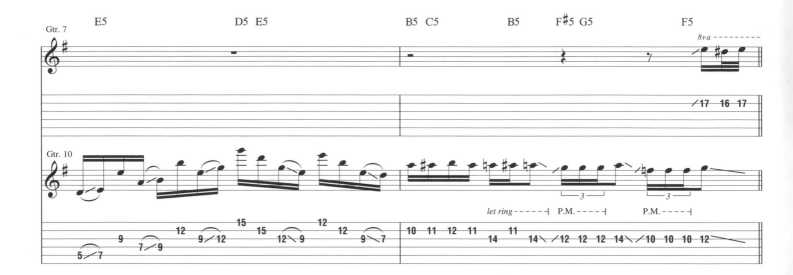

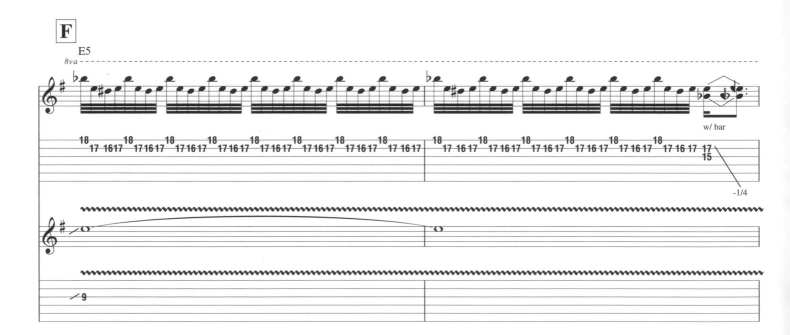

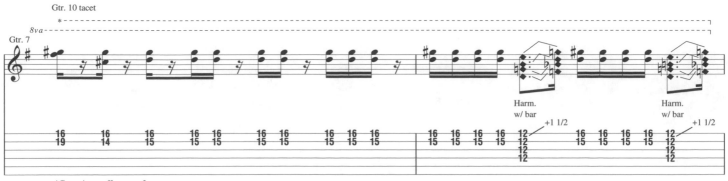

*Gtr. w/ tape effects arr. for gtr.

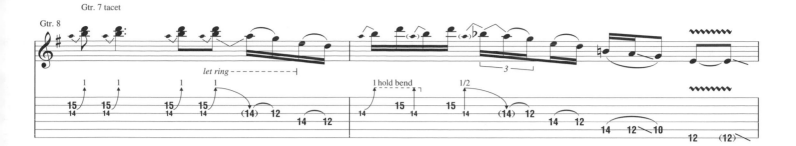

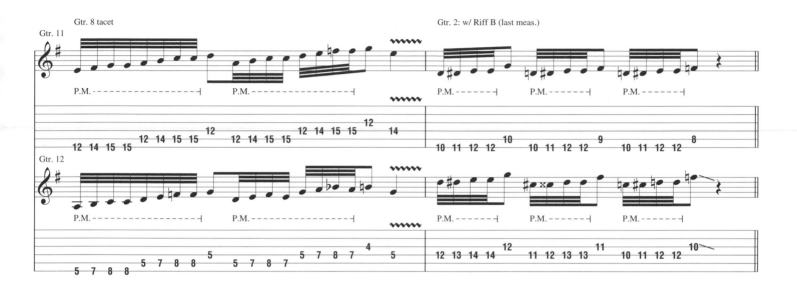

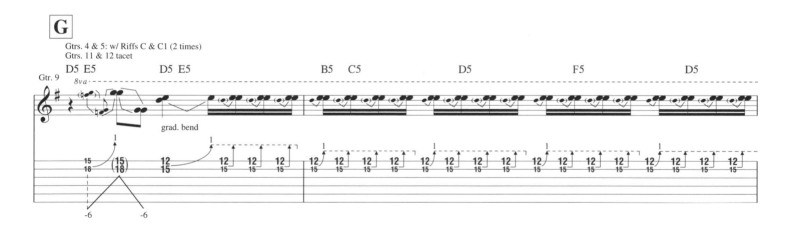

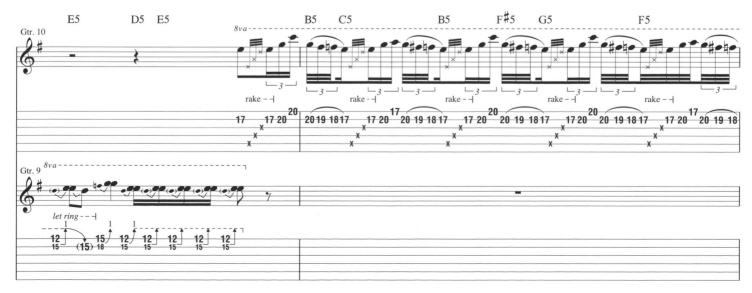

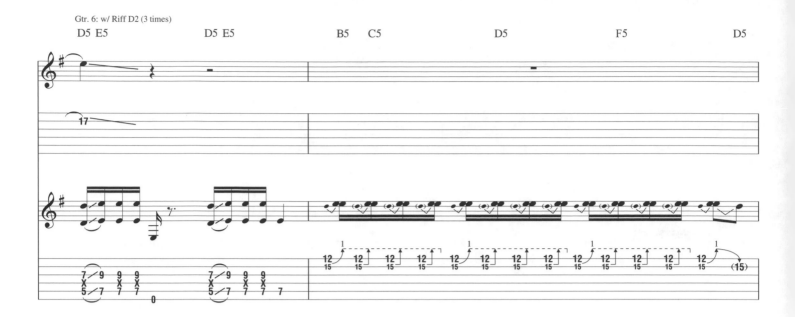

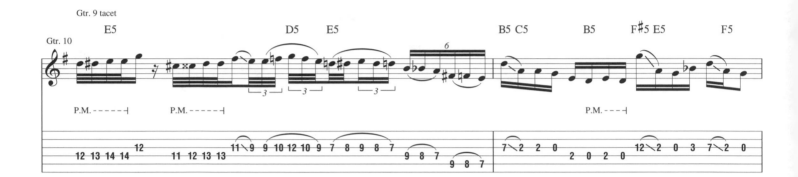

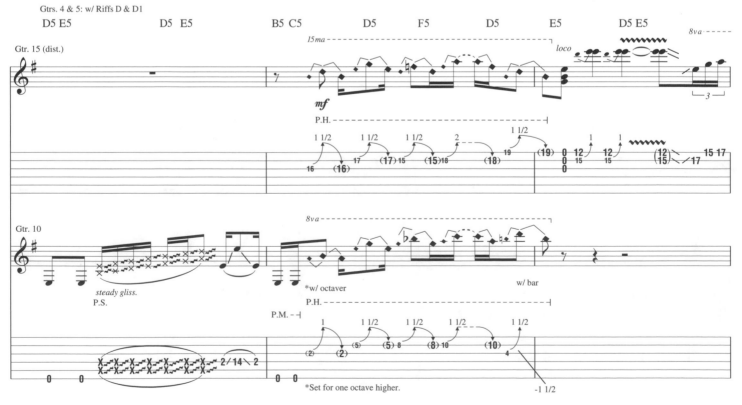

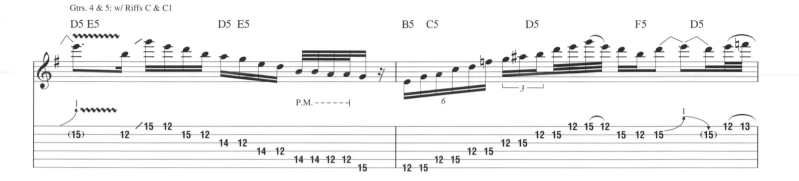

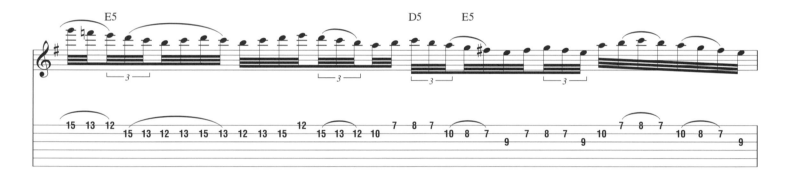

H

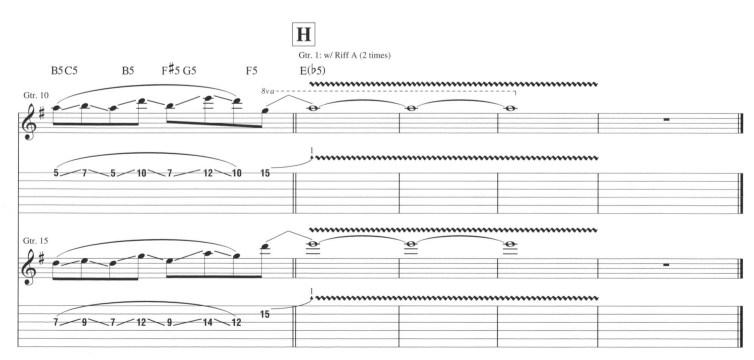

Sweet Georgia Brown

Words and Music by Ben Bernie, Maceo Pinkard and Kenneth Casey

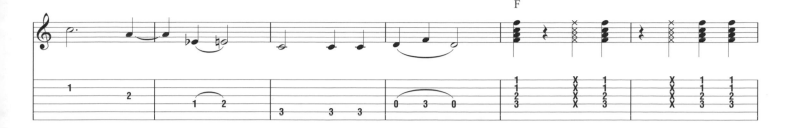

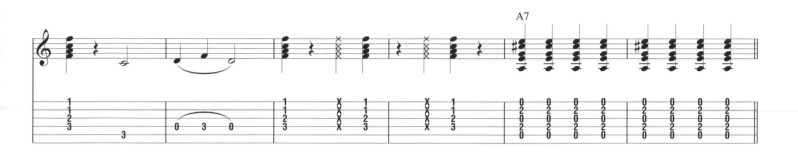

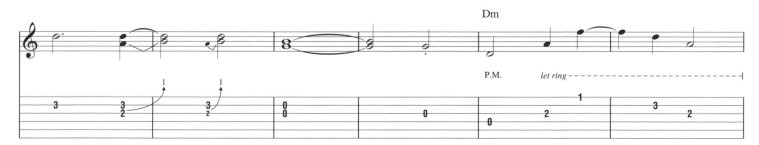

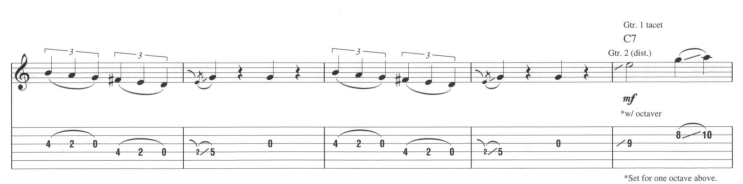

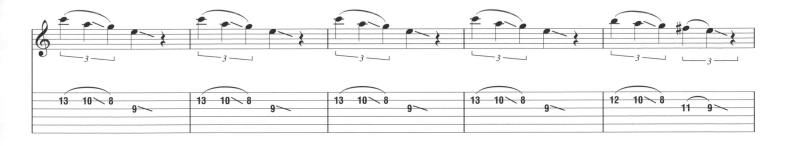

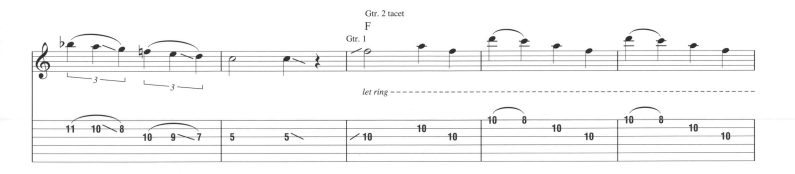

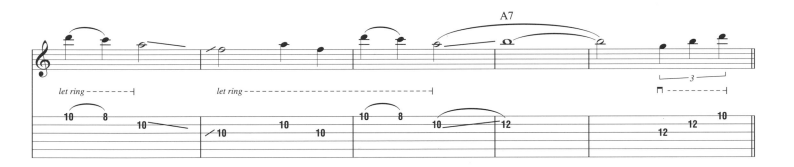

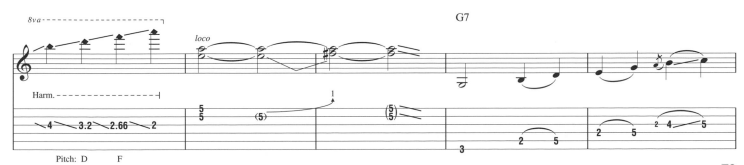

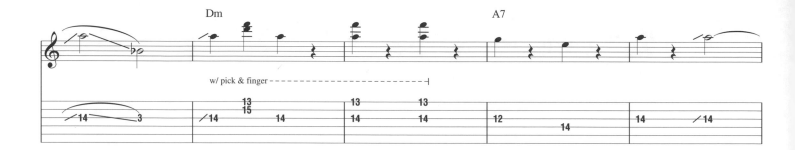

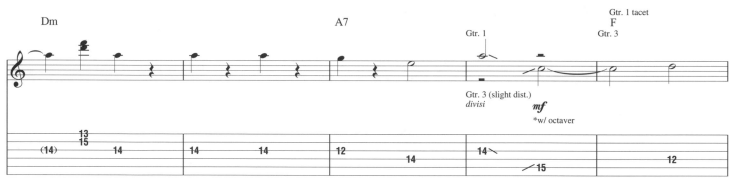

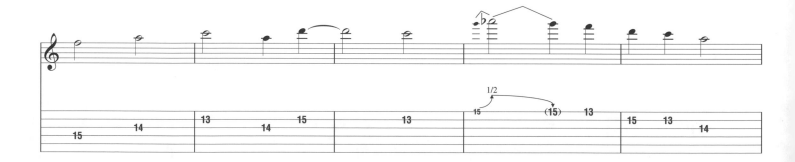

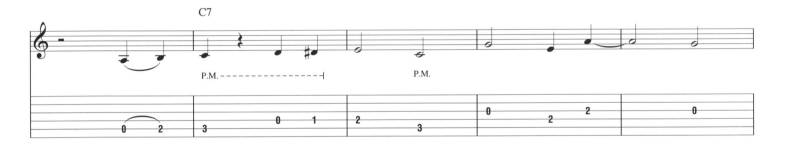
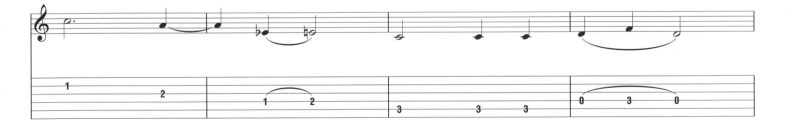

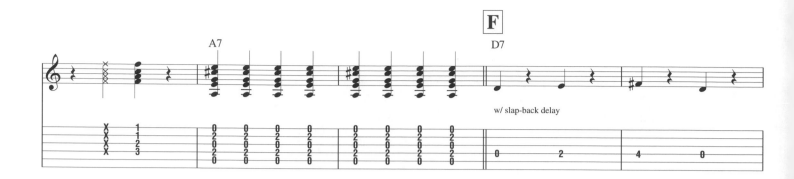

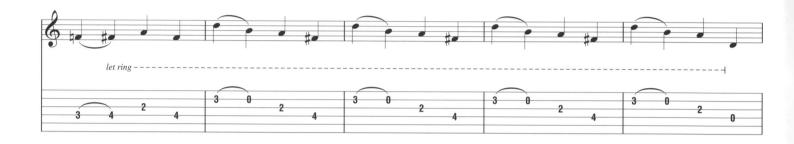

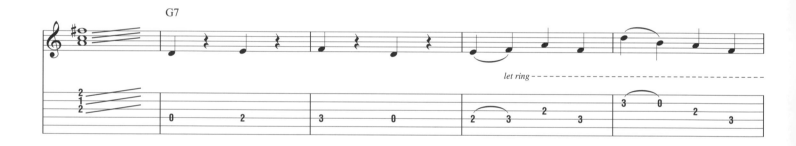

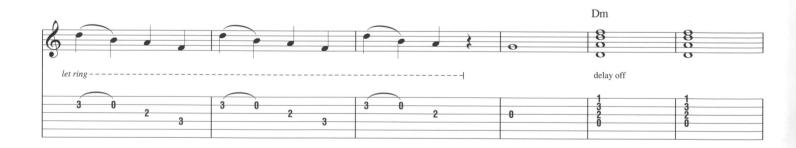

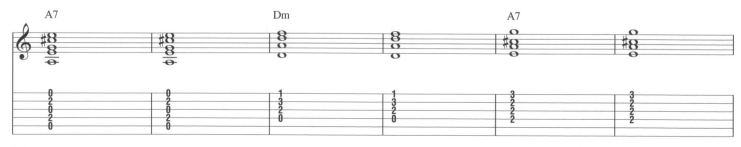

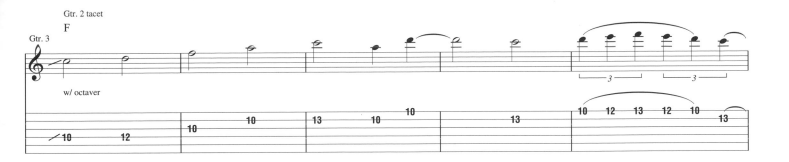

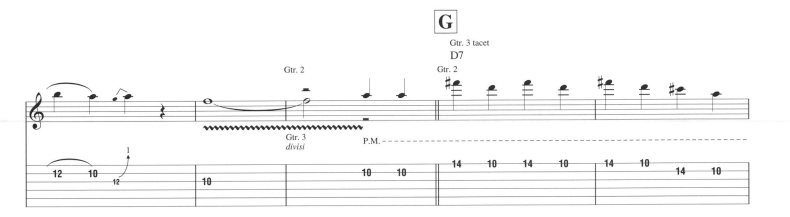

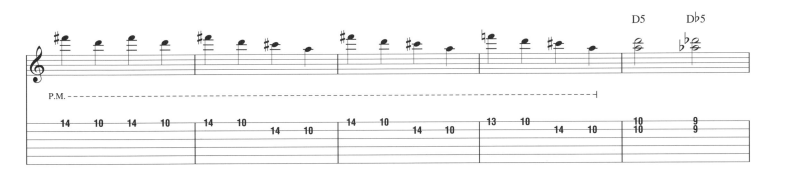

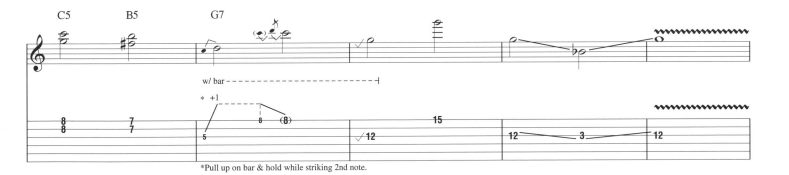

*Pull up on bar & hold while striking 2nd note.

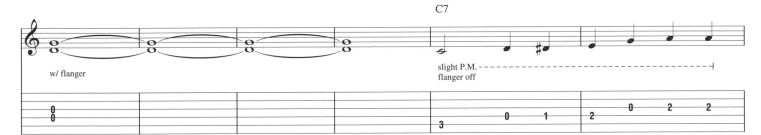

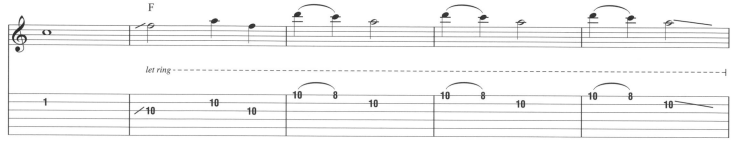

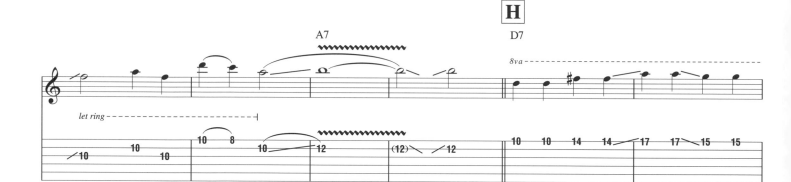

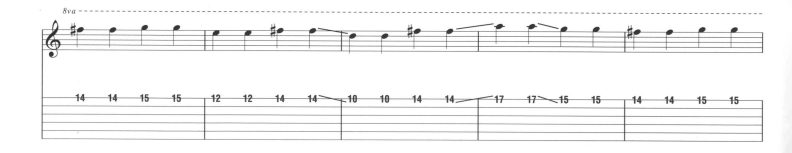

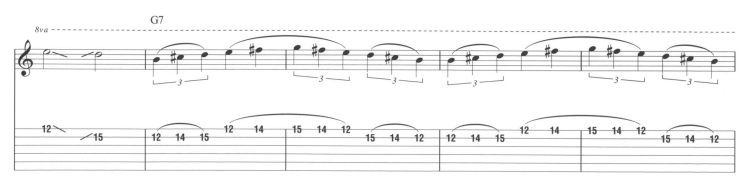

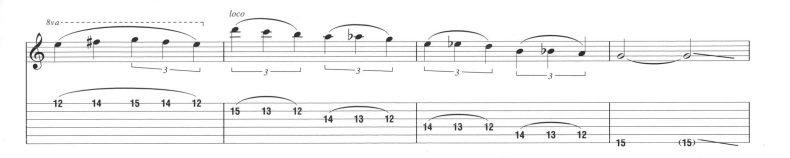

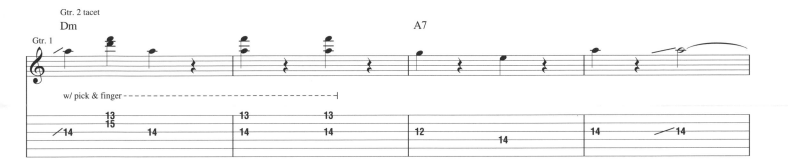

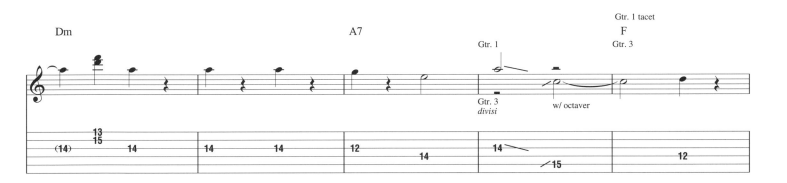

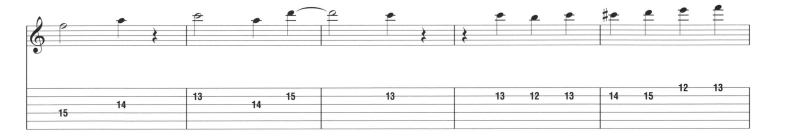

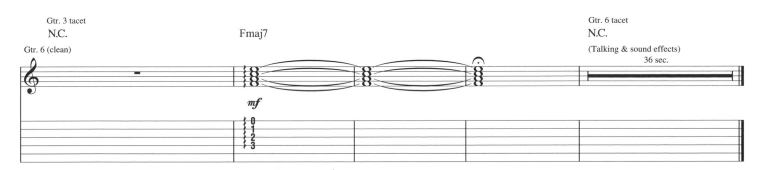

Flatlines, Thin Lines

Music by John 5 and Kevin Savigar

*Chord symbols reflect implied harmony.

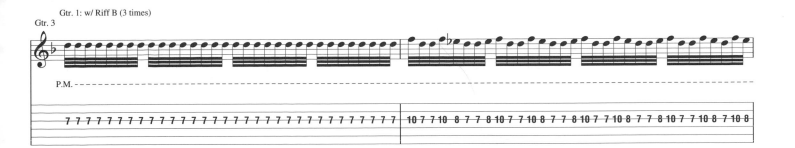

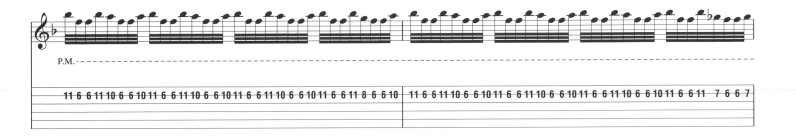

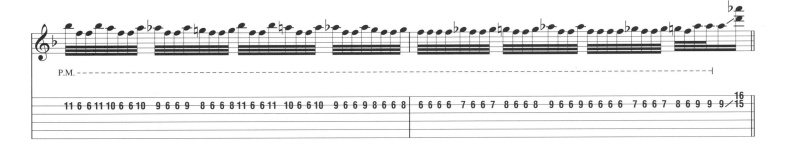

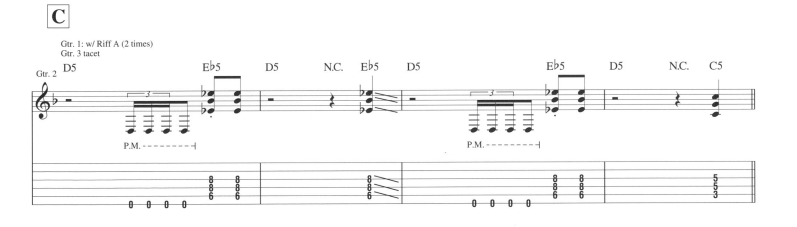

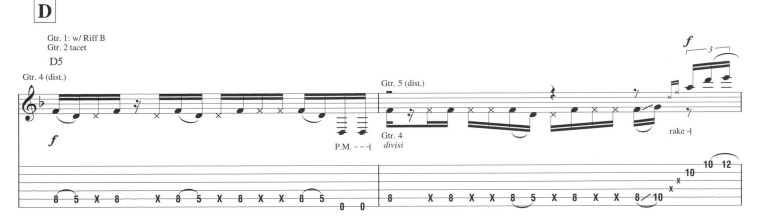

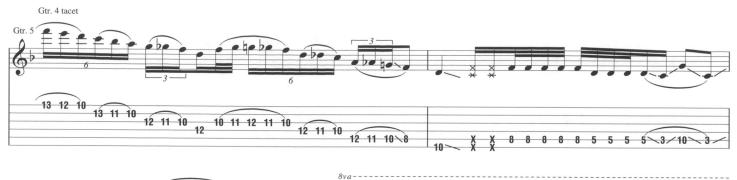

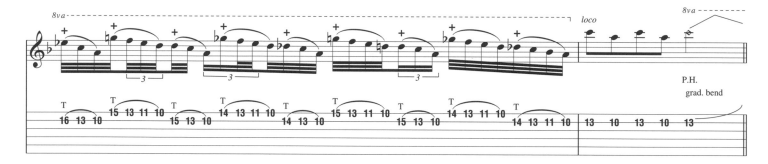

E

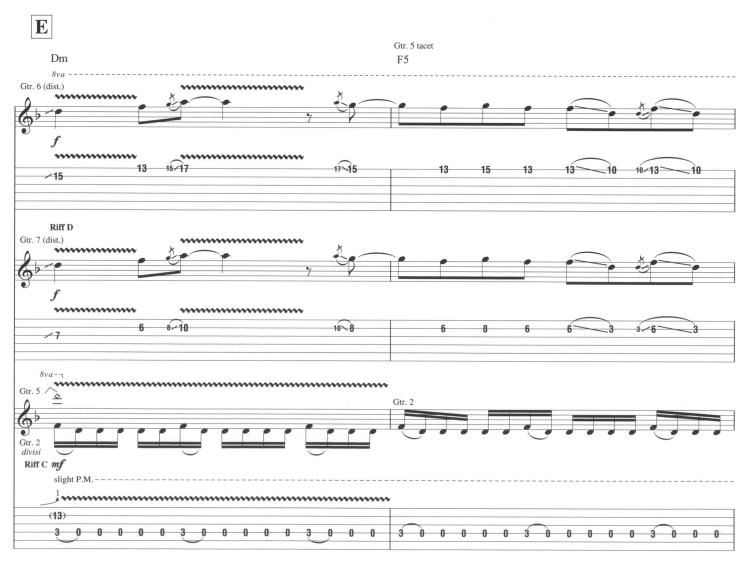

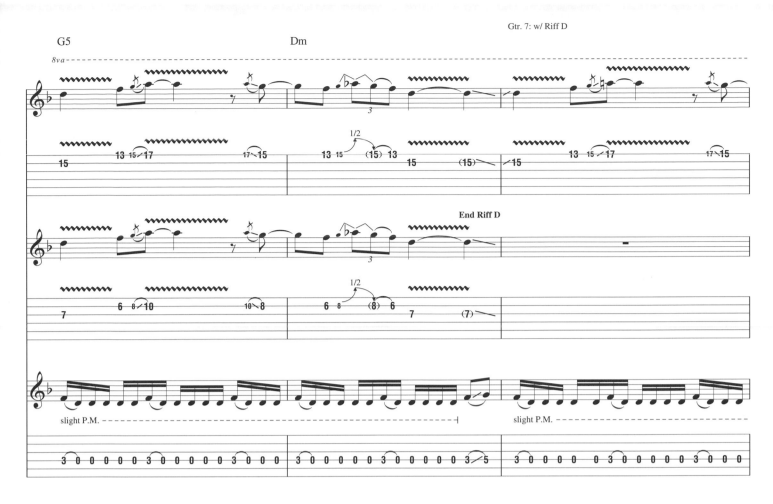

F

Gtr. 1: w/ Riff A (2 times)
Gtr. 6 tacet

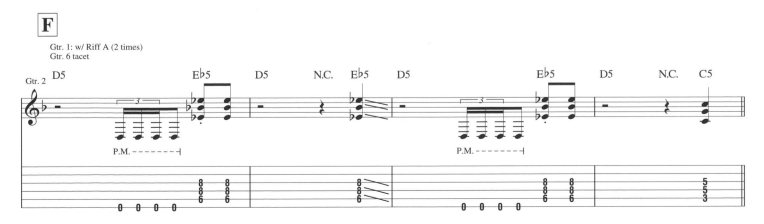

G

Gtr. 1: w/ Riff B (4 times)
Gtr. 2 tacet

Gtr. 3   D5

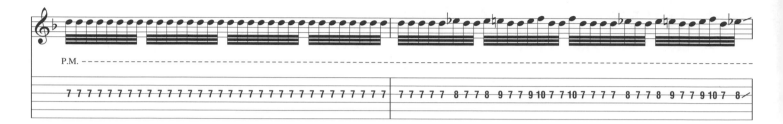

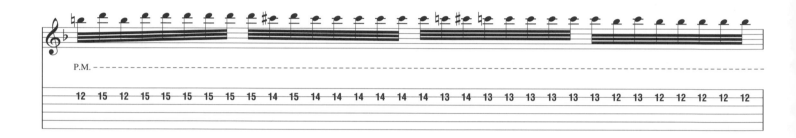

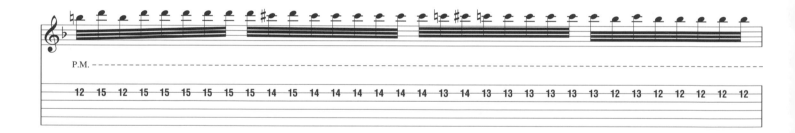

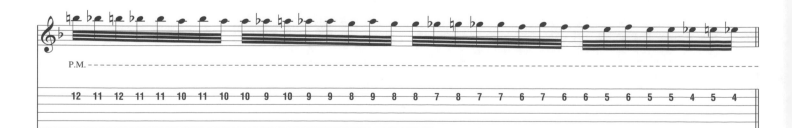

91

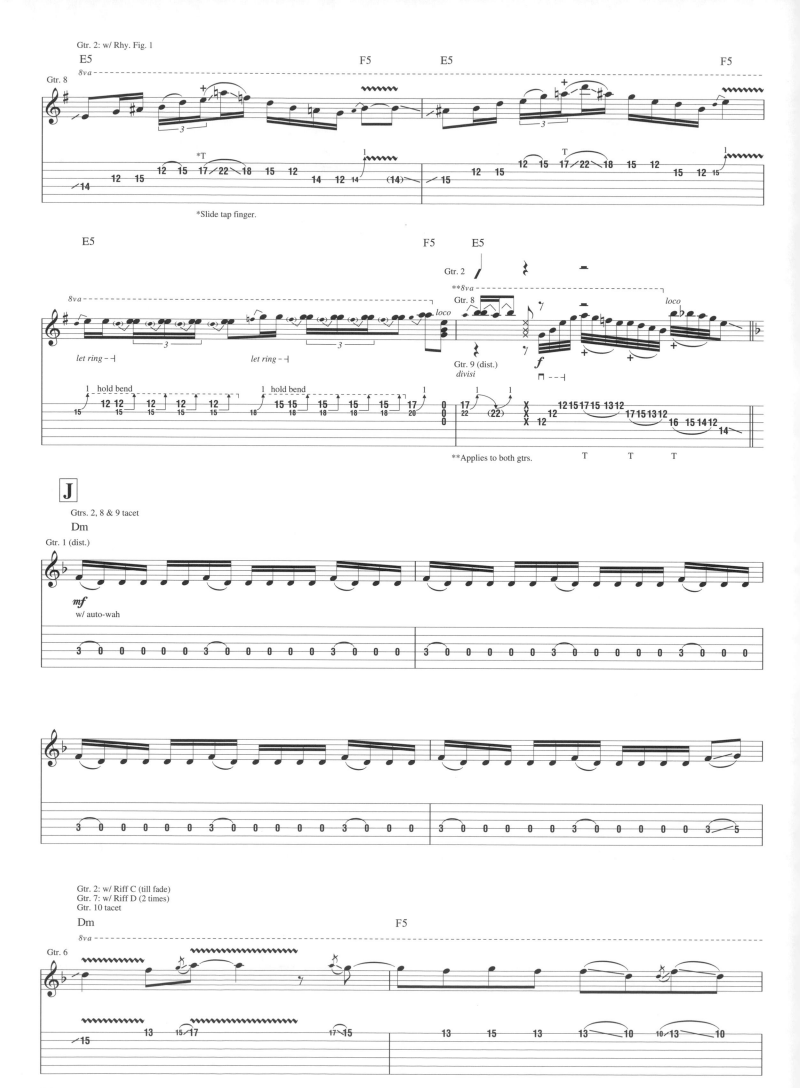

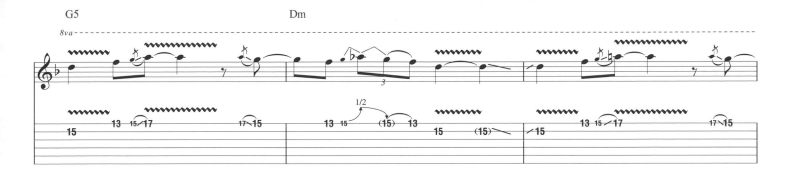

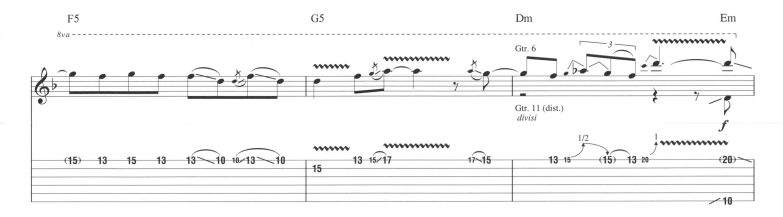

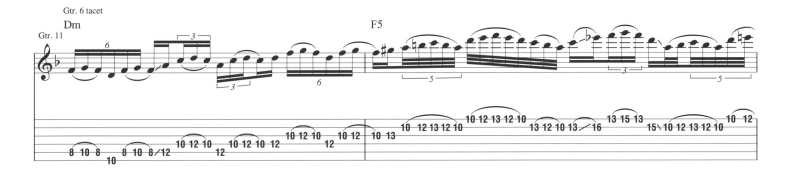

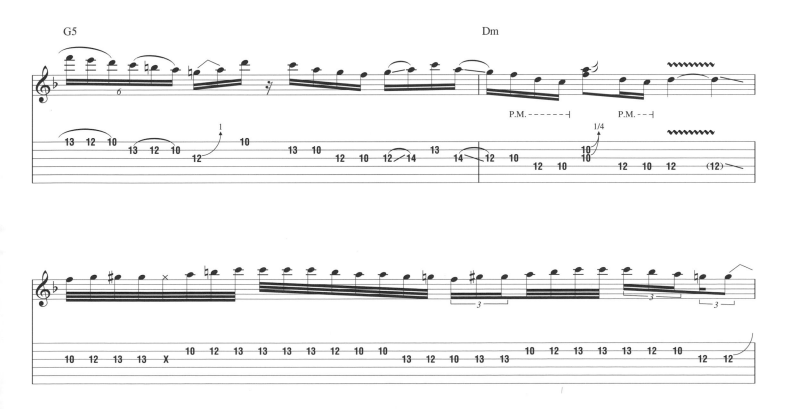

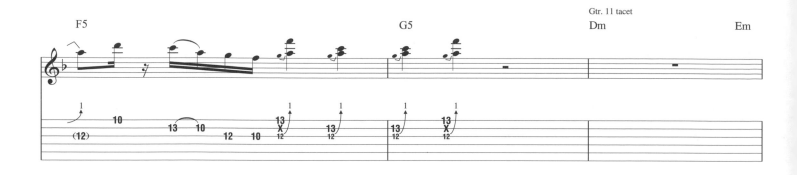

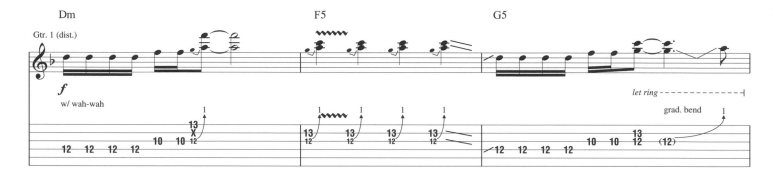

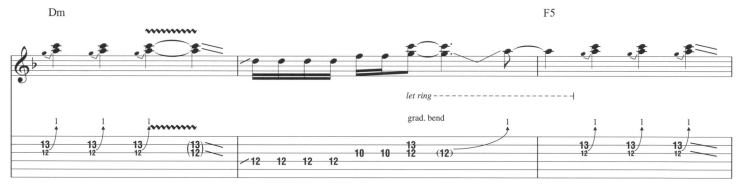

*Bend up and hold while tremolo picking.

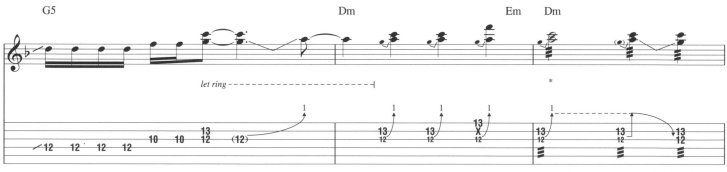

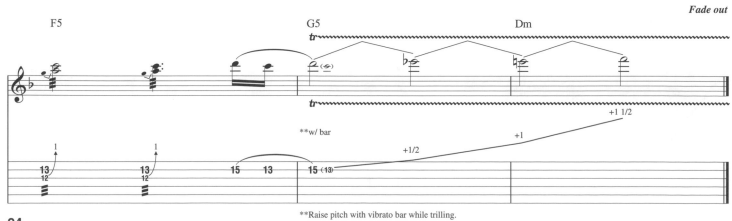

**Raise pitch with vibrato bar while trilling.

Liberty

Music by John 5

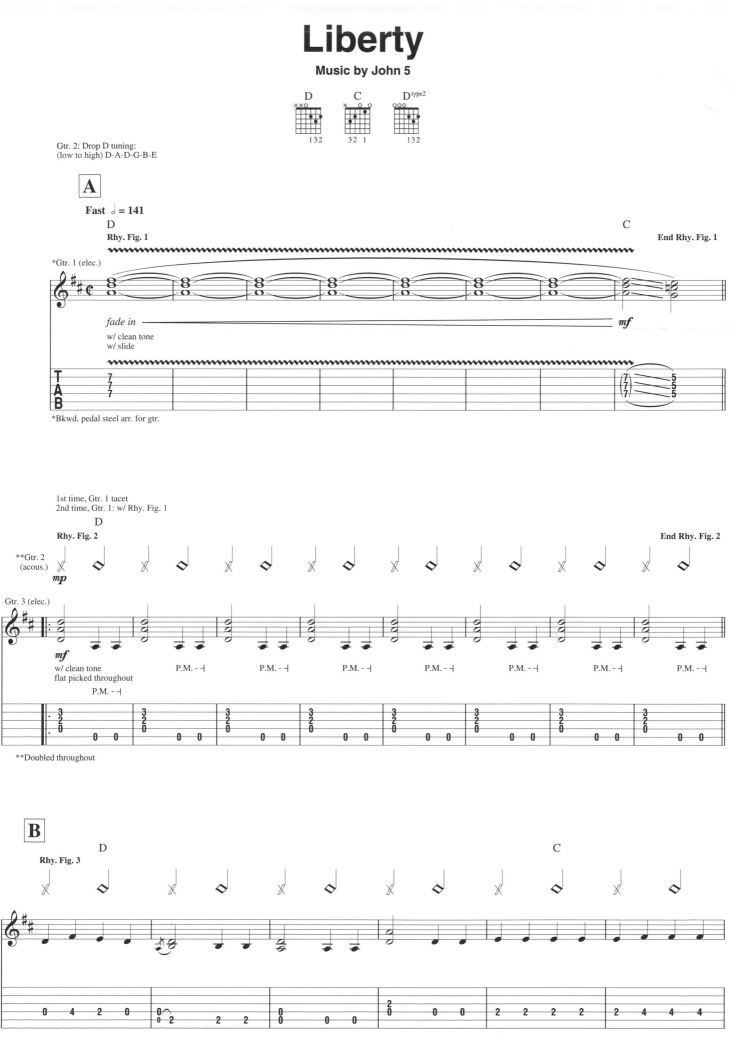

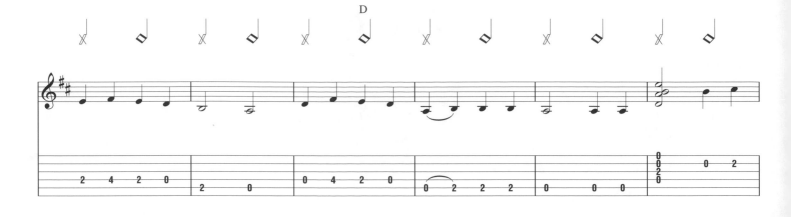

C

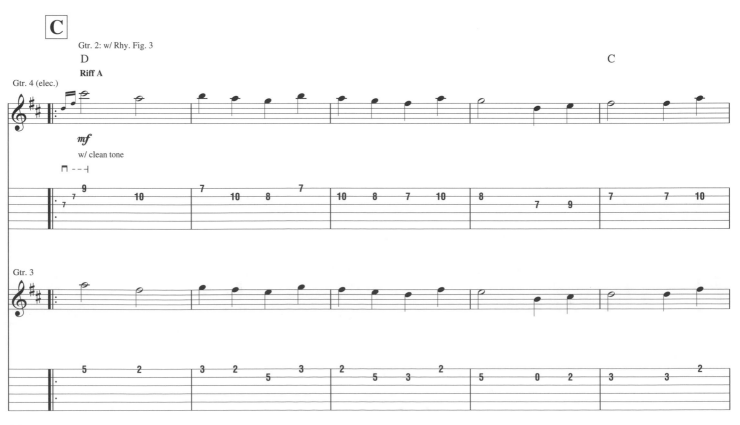

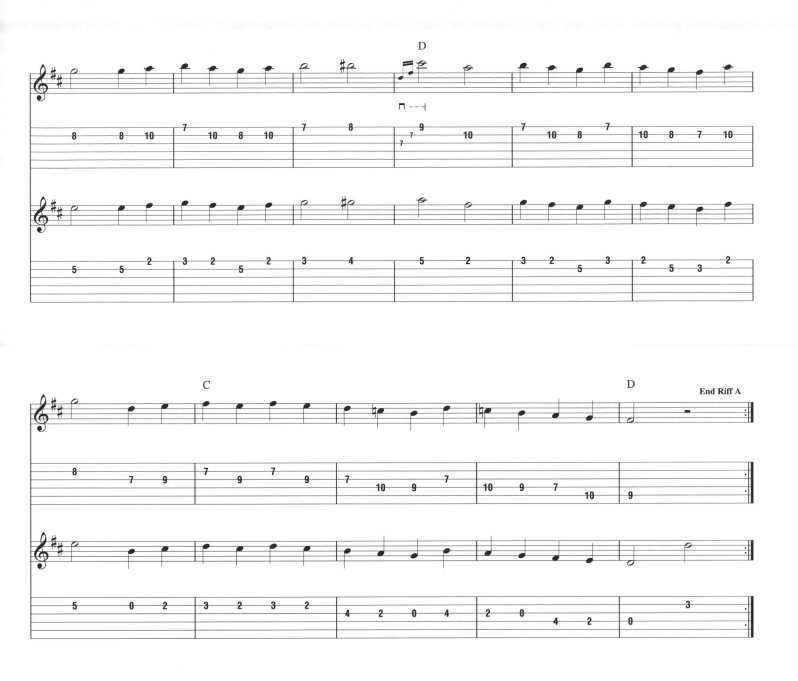

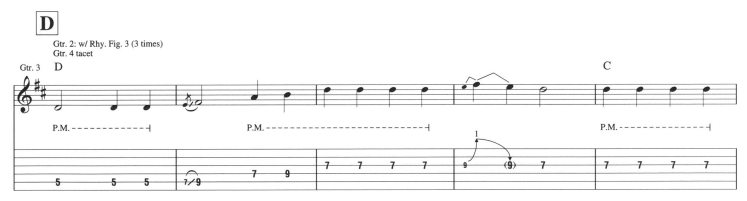

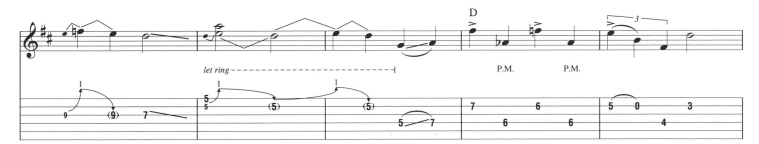

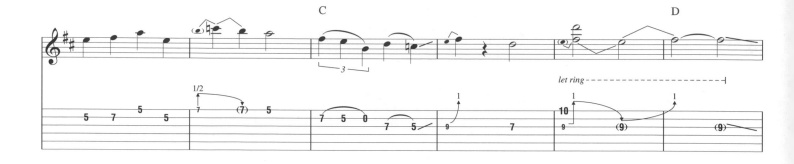

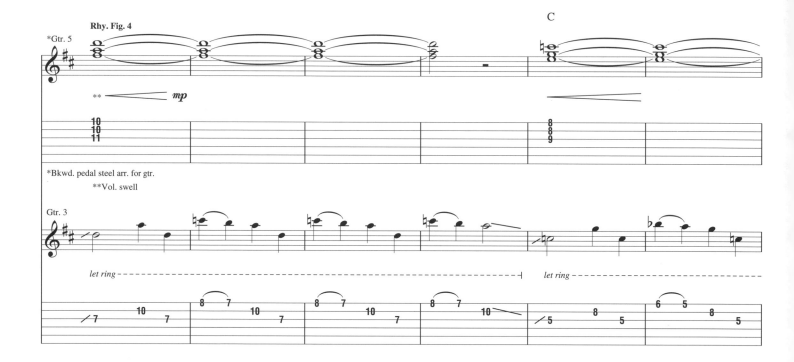

*Bkwd. pedal steel arr. for gtr.

**Vol. swell

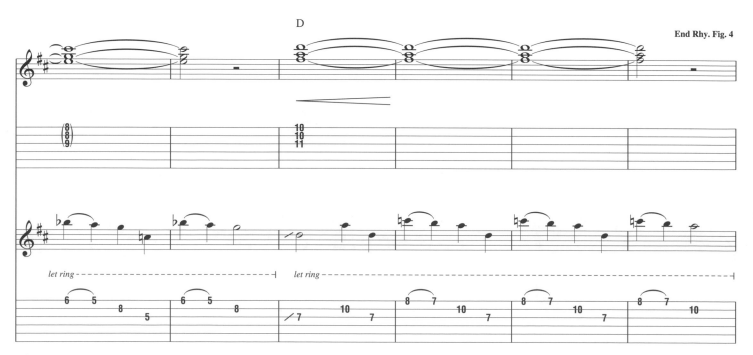

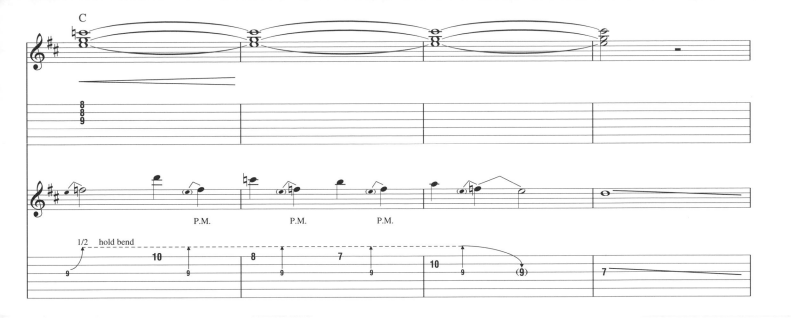

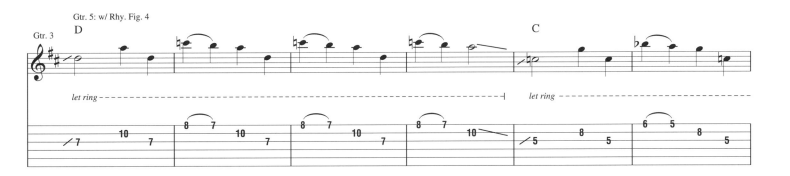

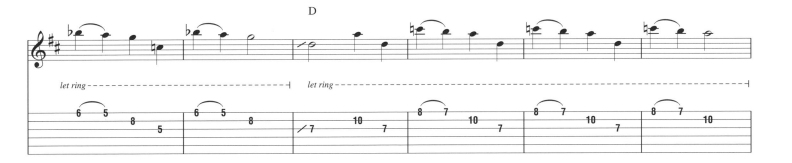

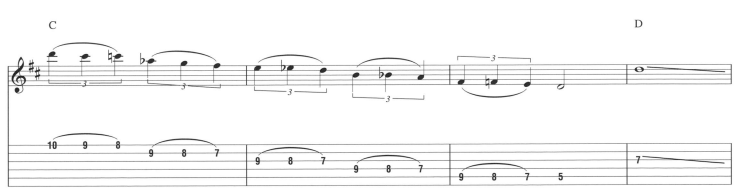

Gtr. 1: w/ Rhy. Fig. 1
Gtr. 2: w/ Rhy. Fig. 2

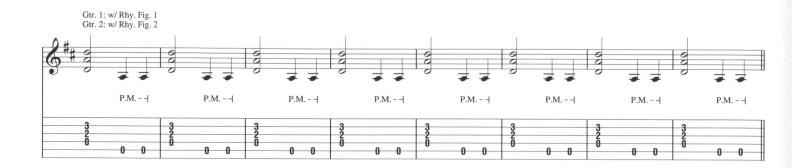

Gtr. 2: w/ Rhy. Fig. 3

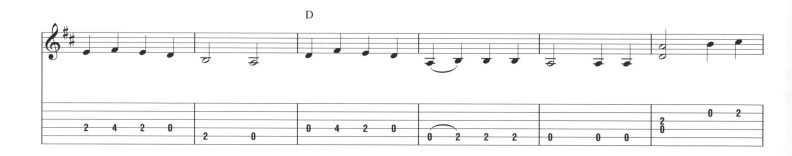

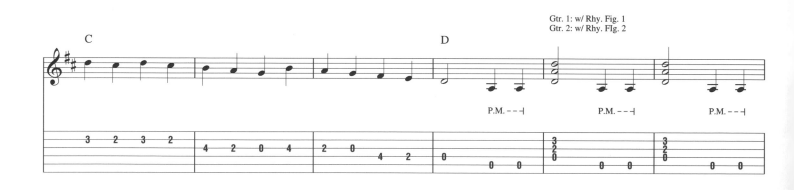

Gtr. 1: w/ Rhy. Fig. 1
Gtr. 2: w/ Rhy. FIg. 2

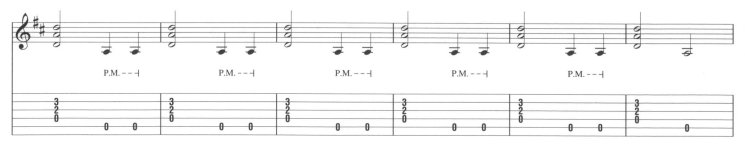

Gtr. 2: w/ Rhy. Fig. 3

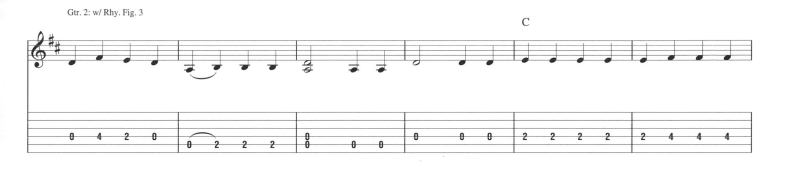

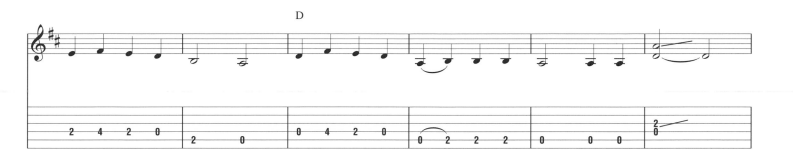

F

Gtr. 2: w/ Rhy. Fig. 3 (2 times)
Gtr. 4: w/ Riff A

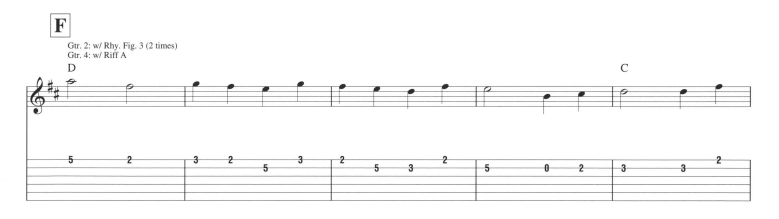

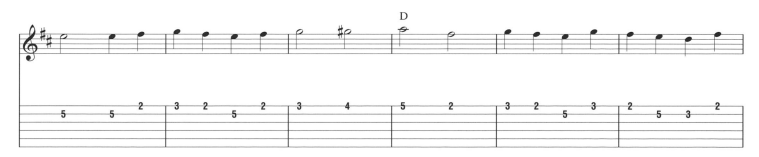

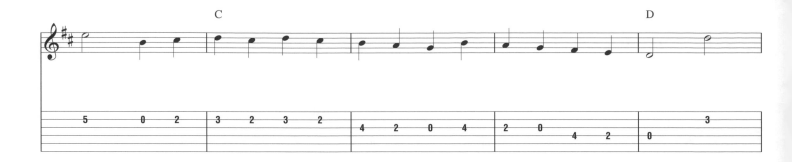

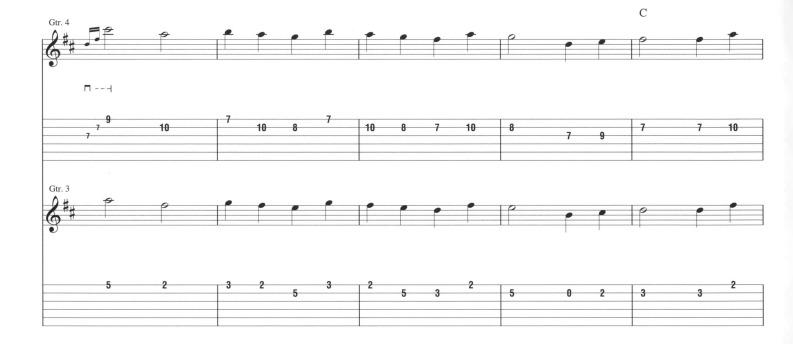

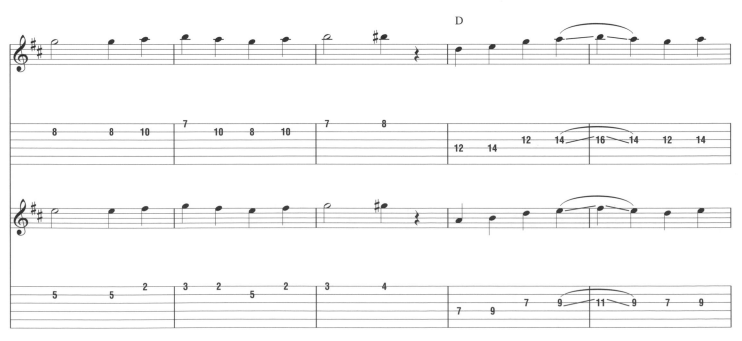

G

Gtr. 2: w/ Rhy. Fig. 3 (1st 12 meas.)
Gtr. 4 tacet

*Press down bar w/ left hand while picking open string with right hand.

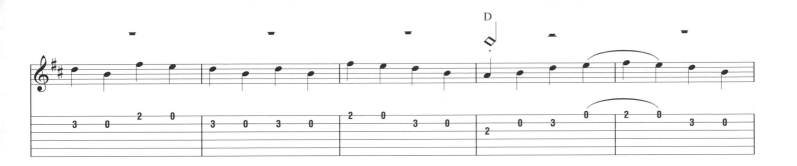

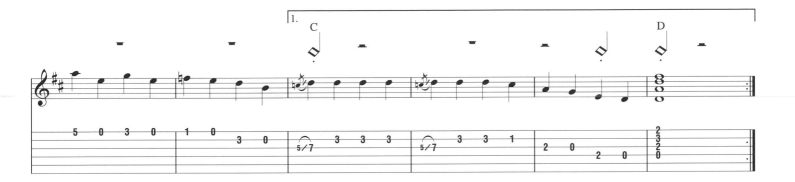

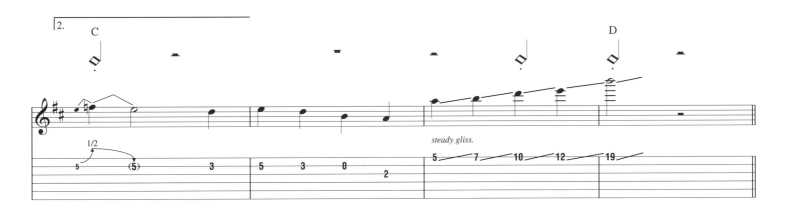

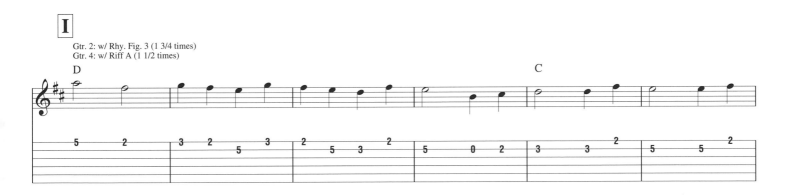

I

Gtr. 2: w/ Rhy. Fig. 3 (1 3/4 times)
Gtr. 4: w/ Riff A (1 1/2 times)

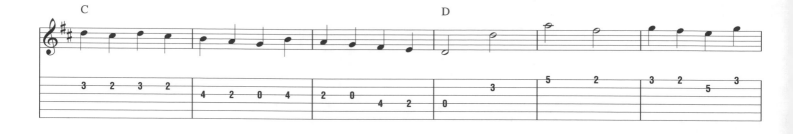

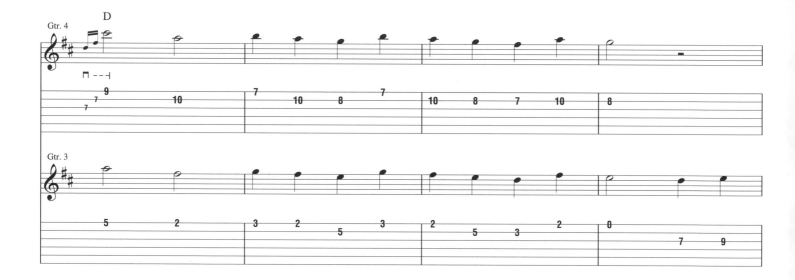

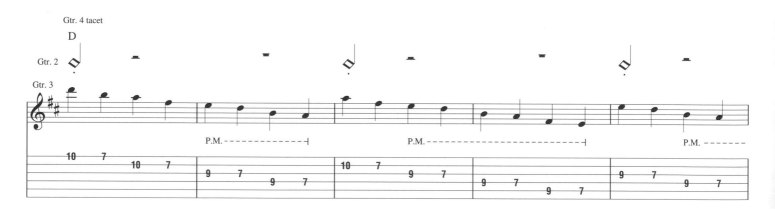

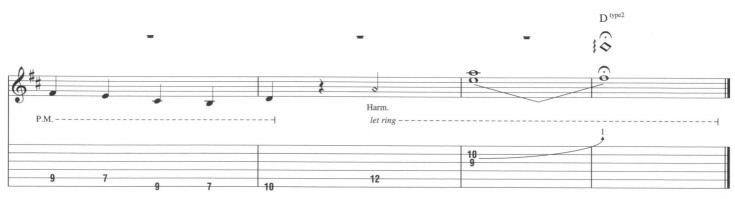

Vertigo

Music by John 5 and Kevin Savigar

Drop B tuning:
(low to high) B-A-D-G-B-E

*Chord symbols reflect overall harmony.
**1st time only
***Set for sixteenth-note regeneration w/ 2 repeats.

†w/ octaver

†Set for one octave lower.

w/ chorus & reverb

Gtr. 3: w/ Riff C

Rhy. Fig. 1

*Two gtrs. arr. for one.

B

Gtrs. 1, 2 & 3: w/ Riffs A, B & C (2 times)
Gtr. 4: w/ Rhy. Fig. 1 (2 times)

B5

End Rhy. Fig. 1

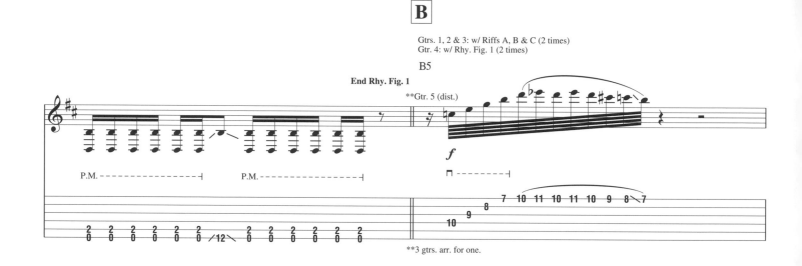

**Gtr. 5 (dist.)

**3 gtrs. arr. for one.

***Gtr. 6 (dist.)

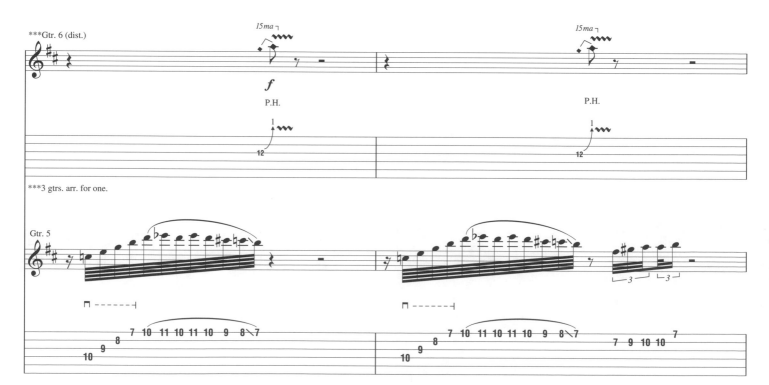

***3 gtrs. arr. for one.

Gtr. 5

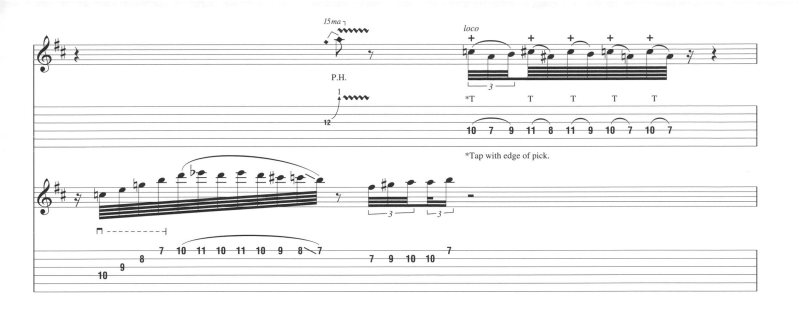

*Tap with edge of pick.

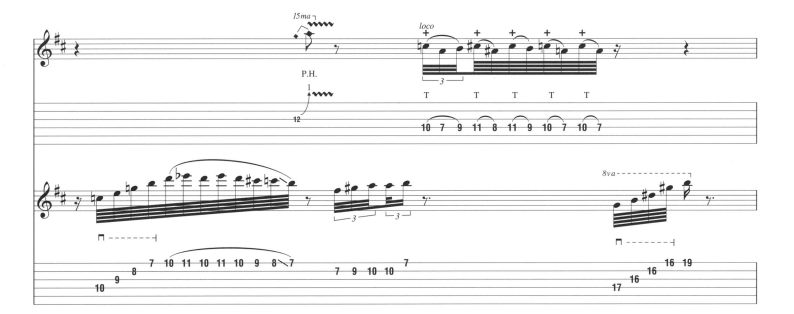

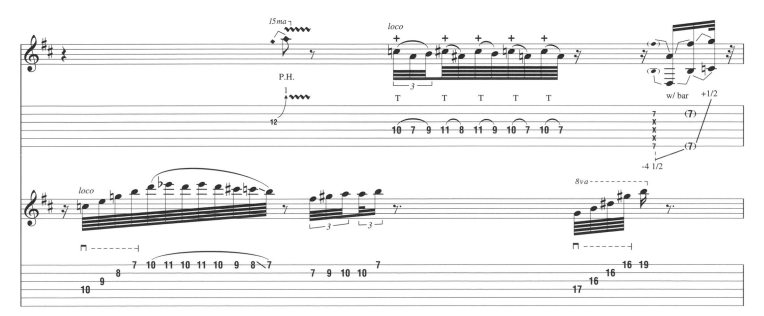

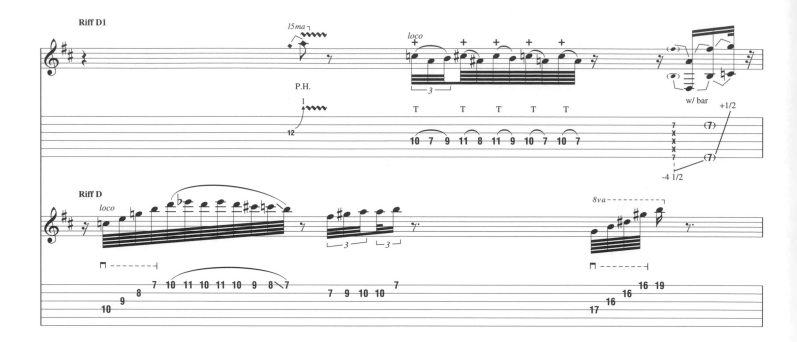

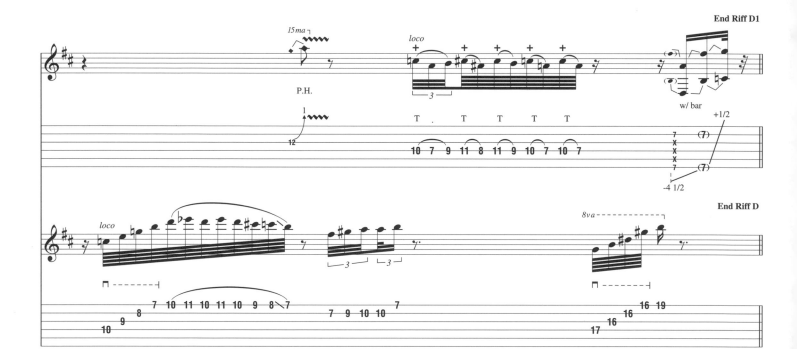

C

Gtrs. 5 & 6 tacet

B5

Gtr. 1

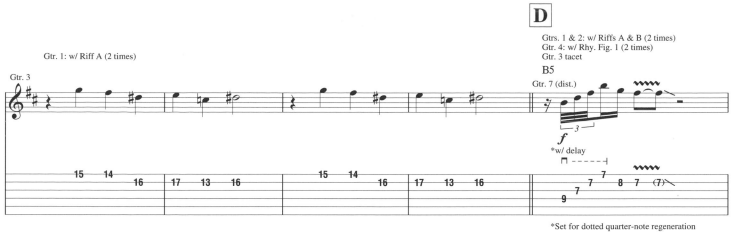

*Set for dotted quarter-note regeneration
w/ 2 repeats.

**Set for quarter-note regeneration w/ 2 repeats.

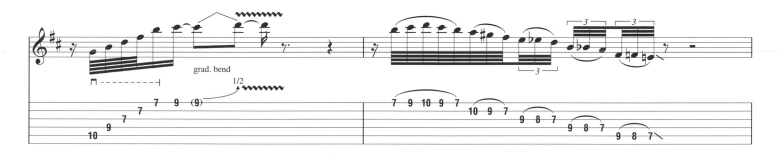

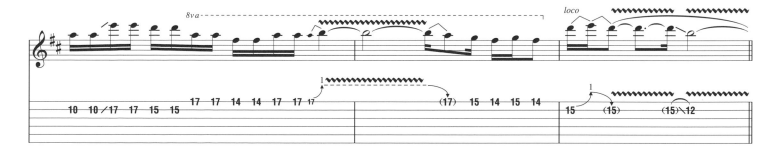

***w/ increasing signal distortion.

18969 Ventura Blvd.

Music by John 5 and Kevin Savigar

*Chord symbols reflect implied harmony.

**T=Thumb on 6th string.

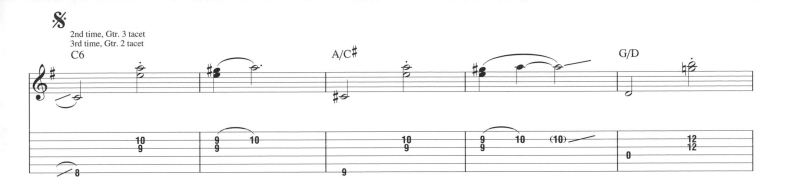

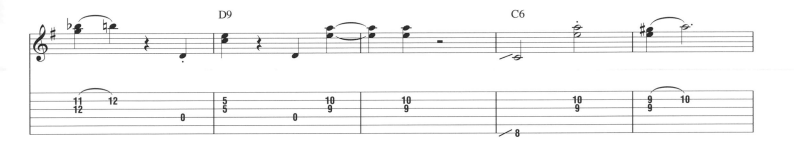

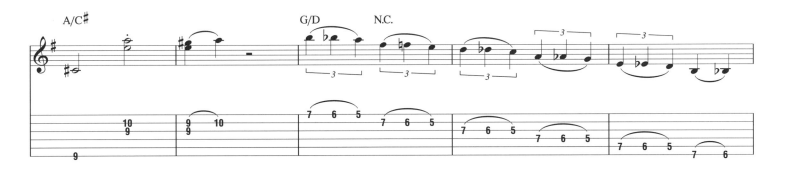

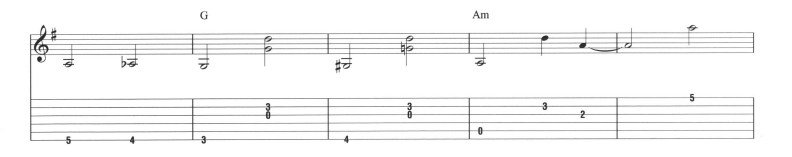

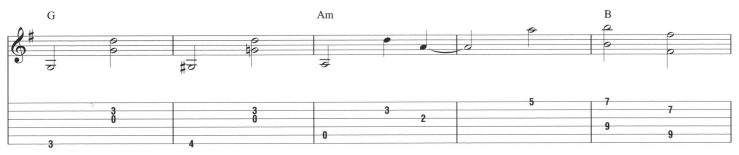

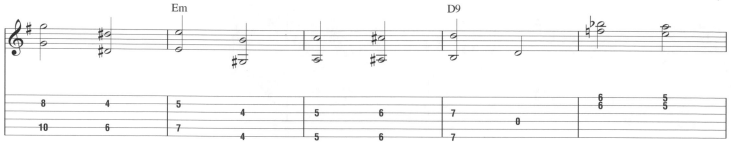

B

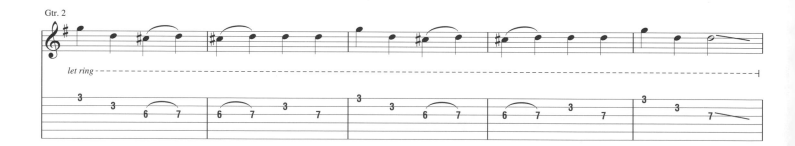

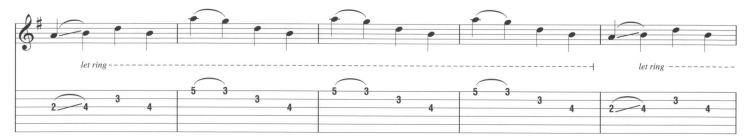

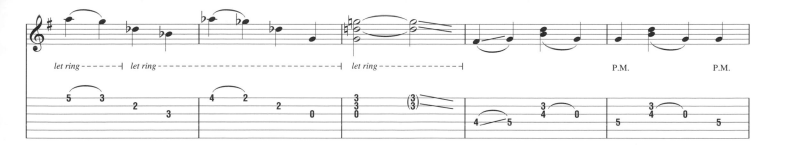

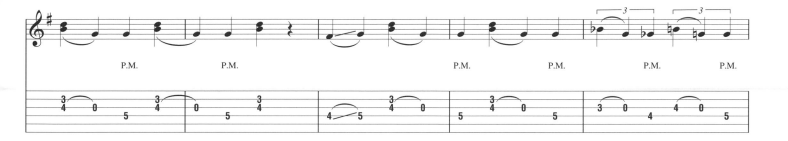

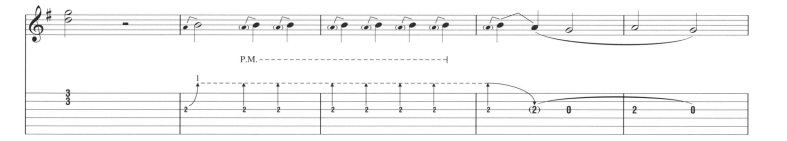

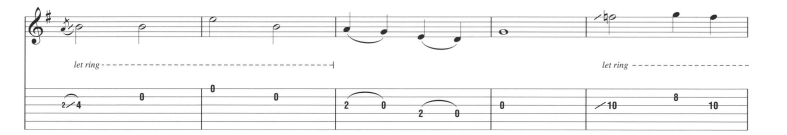

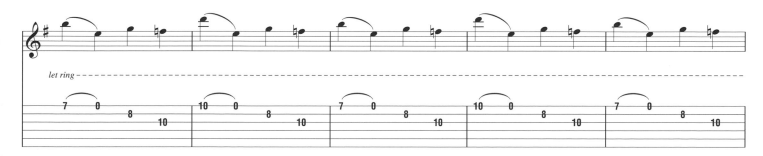

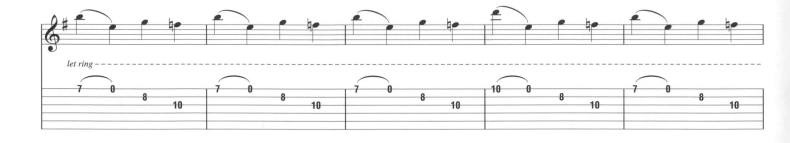

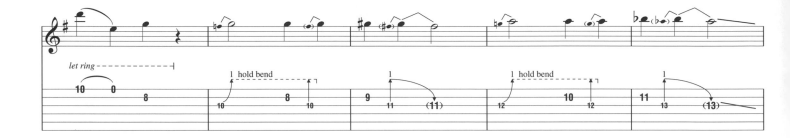

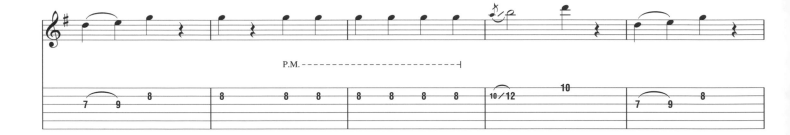

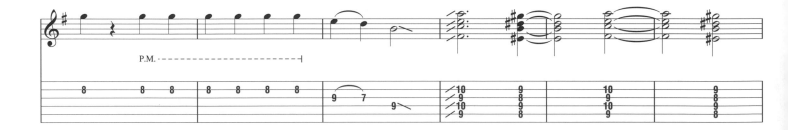

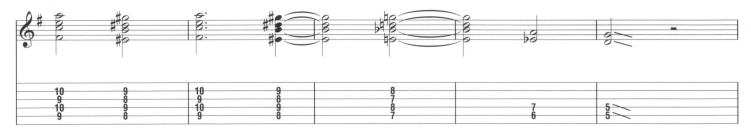

116

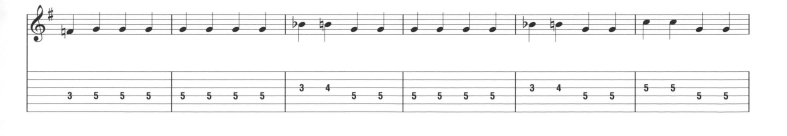

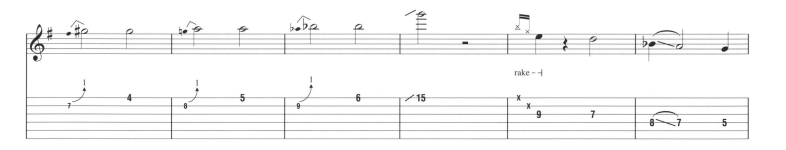

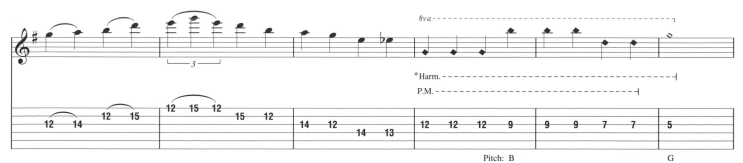

Pitch: B   G
*Gradually slide fret hand towards headstock while playing harmonics.

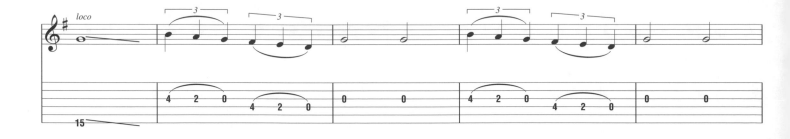

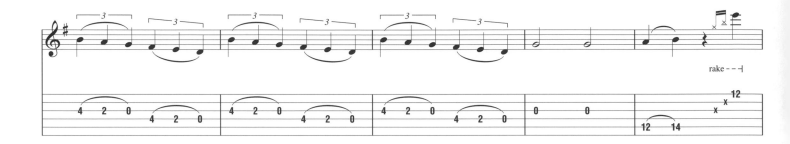

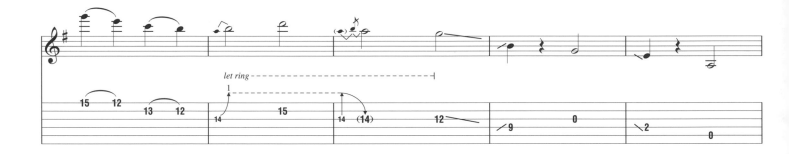

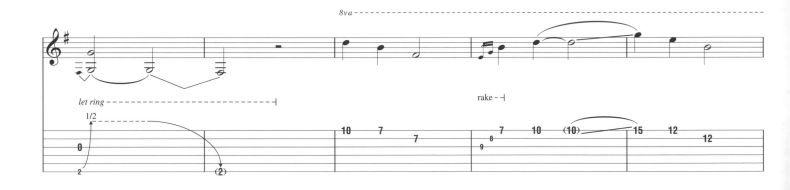

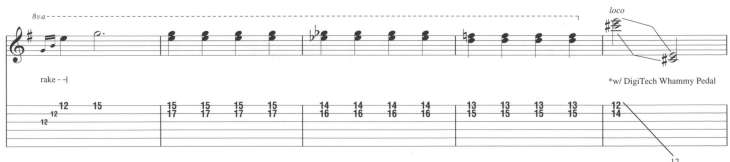

*Set for two octaves below.

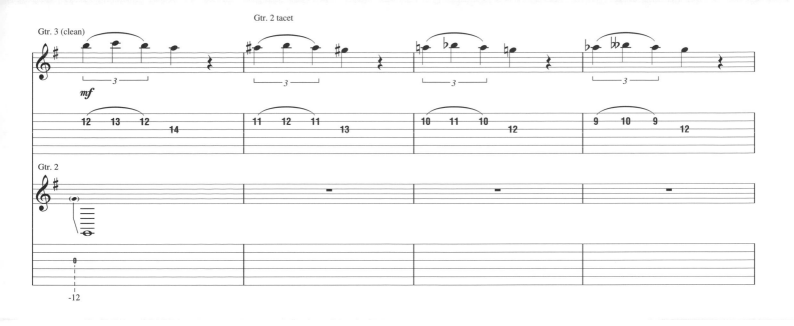

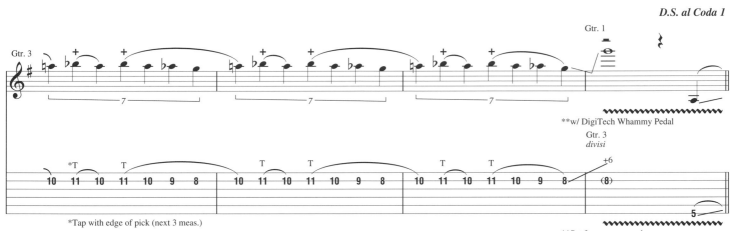

**w/ DigiTech Whammy Pedal

*Tap with edge of pick (next 3 meas.)

**Set for one octave above.

Coda 1

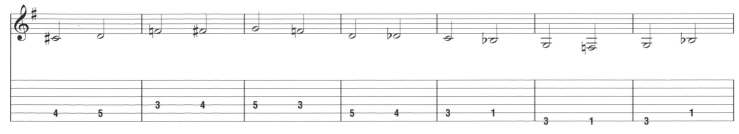

***Acous. bass arr. for gtr.

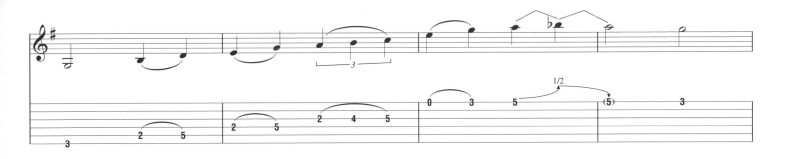

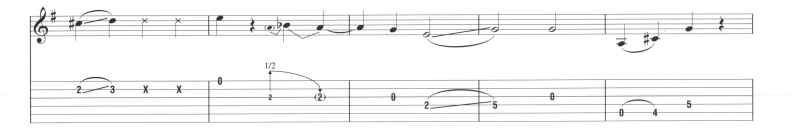

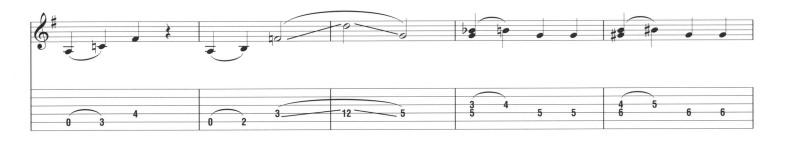

*Steady glissando up the neck.
Pitches are approximate.

D.S. al Coda 2   ⊕ **Coda 2**

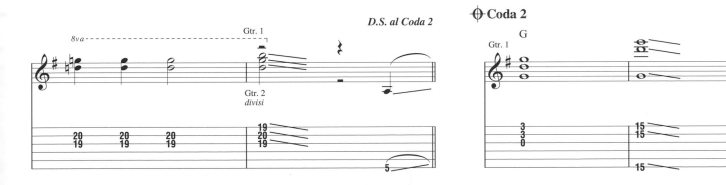

Zugg Island Convict

Music by John 5, Kevin Savigar and J.T. Harding

*Chord symbols reflect basic harmony.

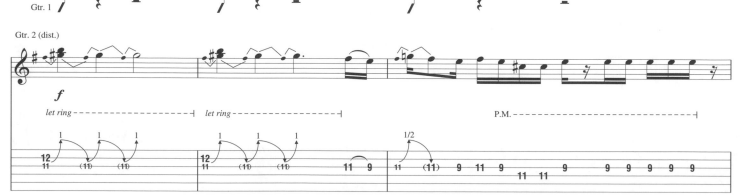

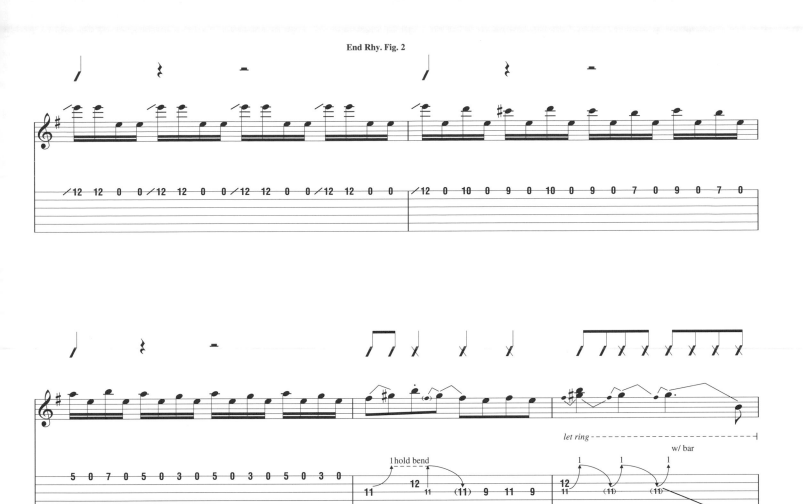

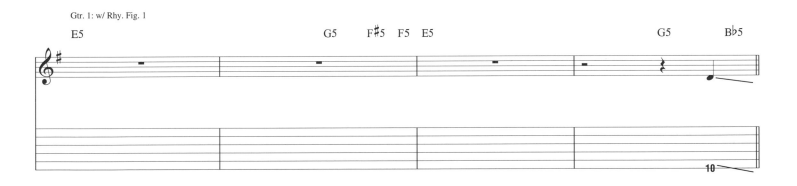

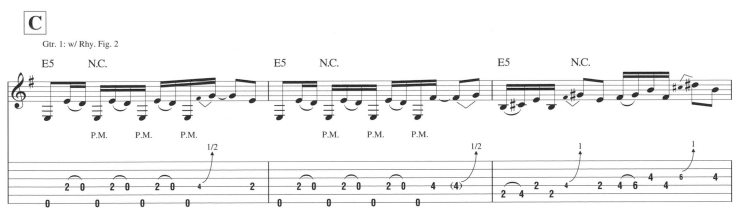

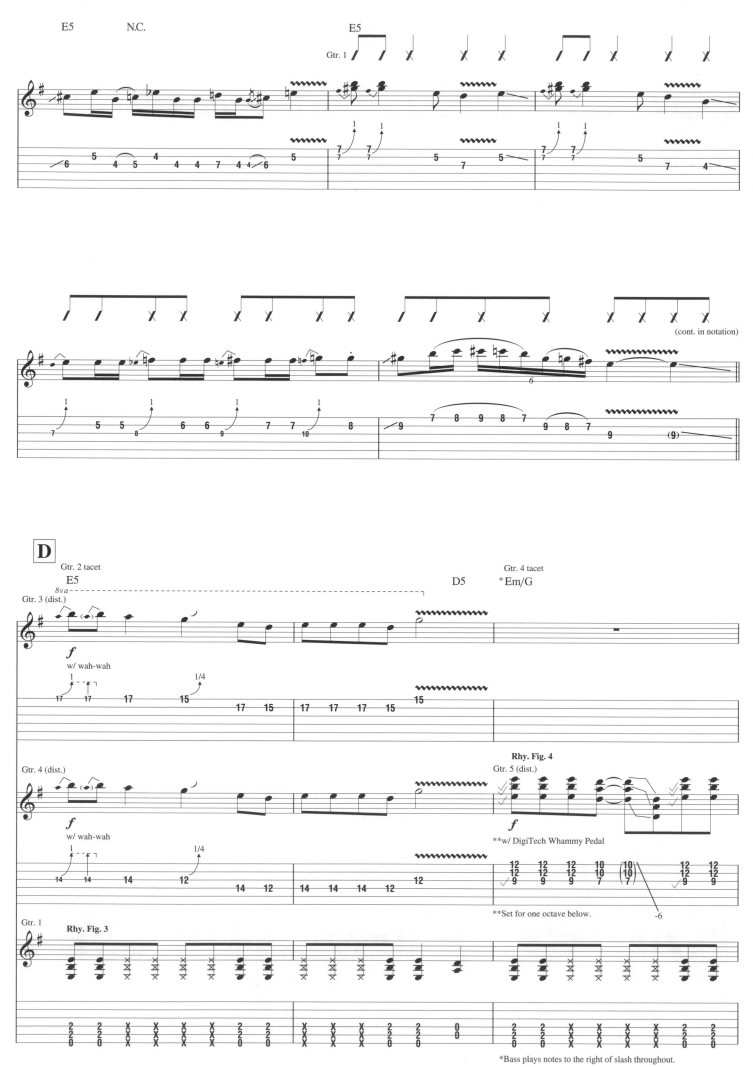

*Bass plays notes to the right of slash throughout.

124

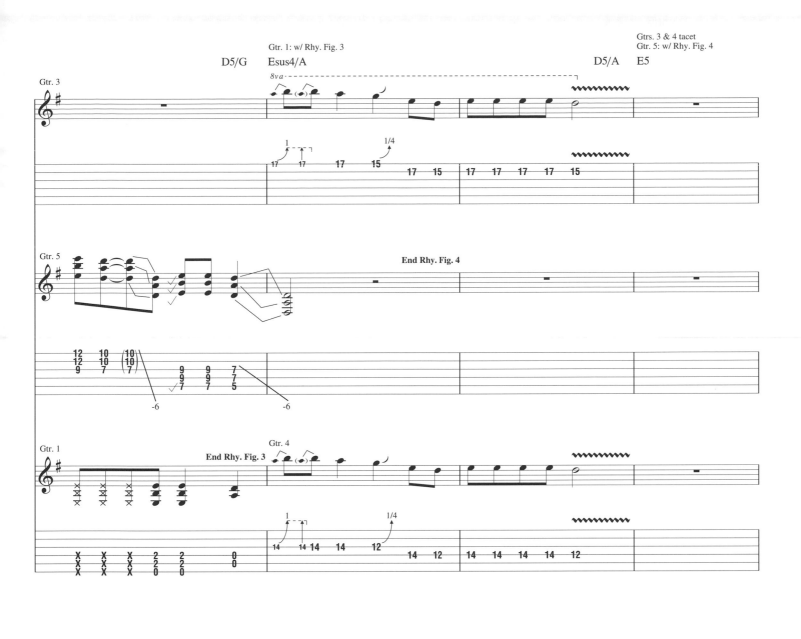

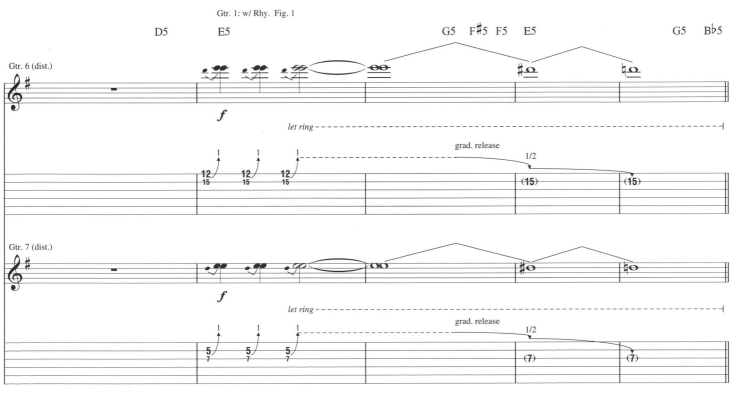

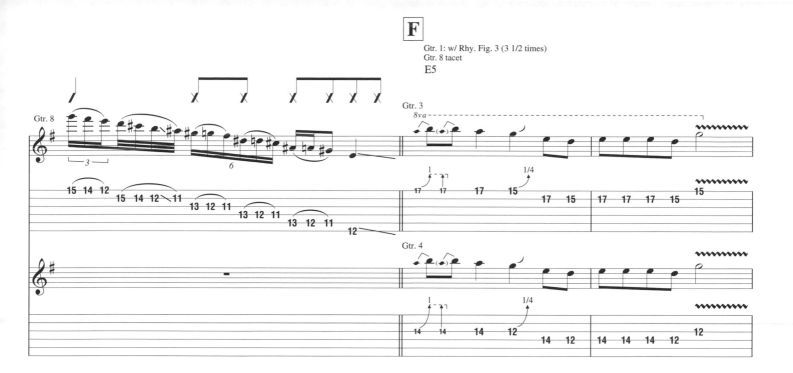

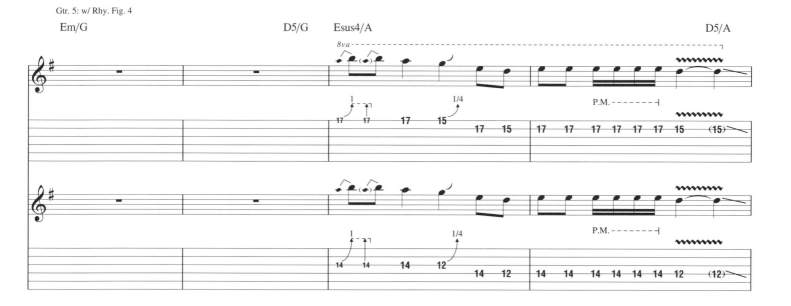

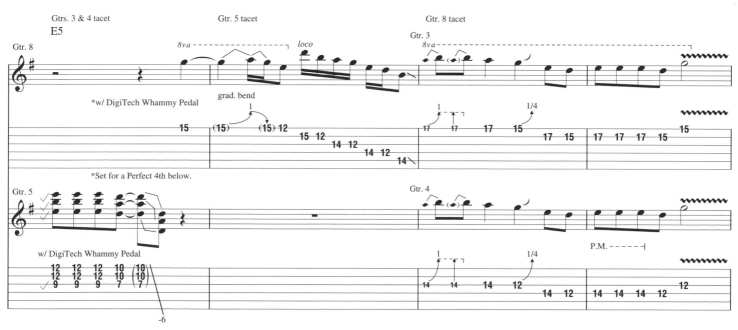

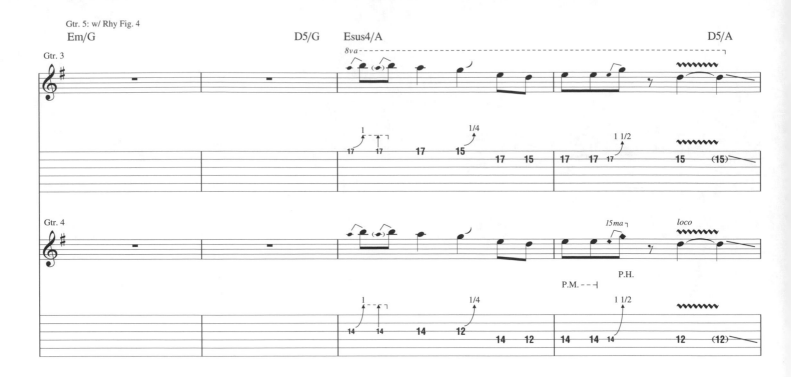

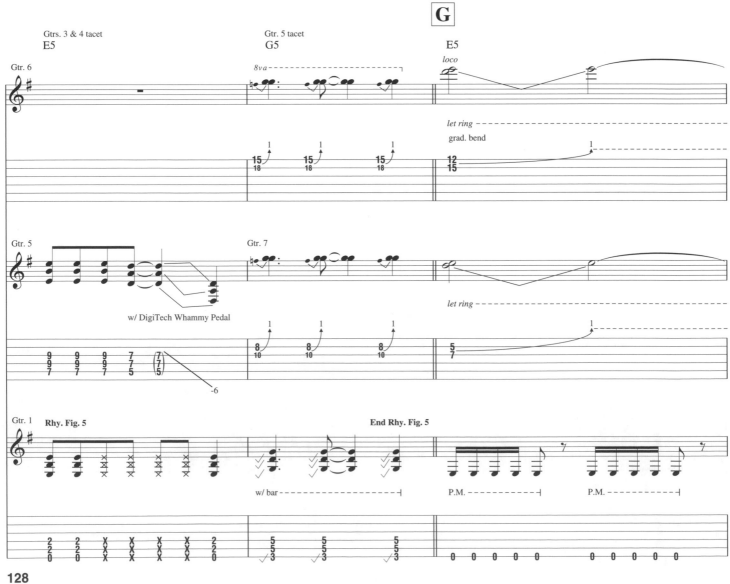

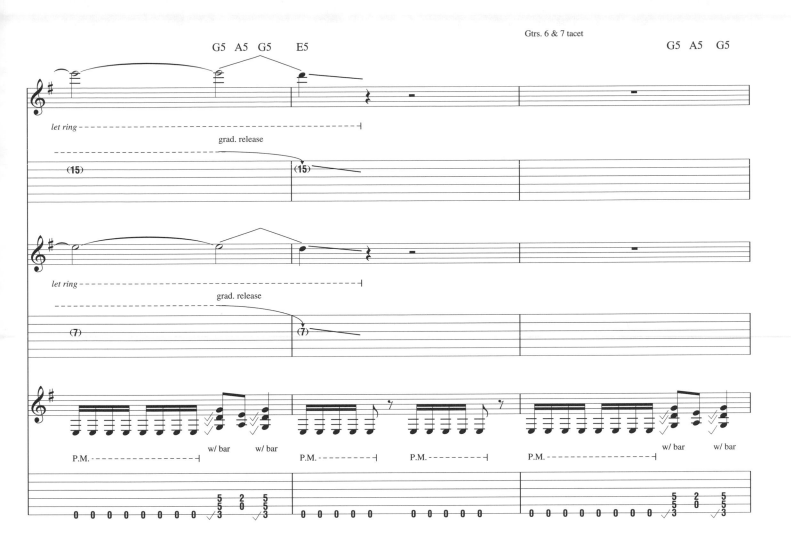

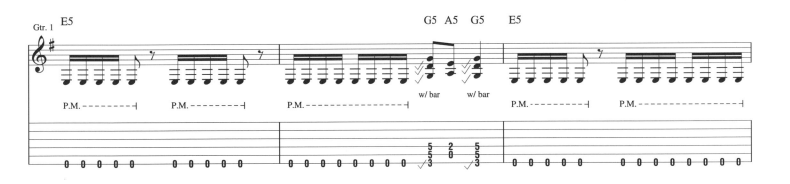

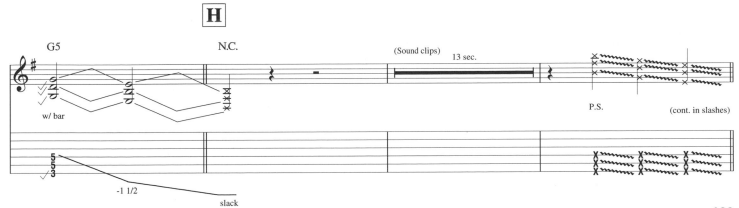

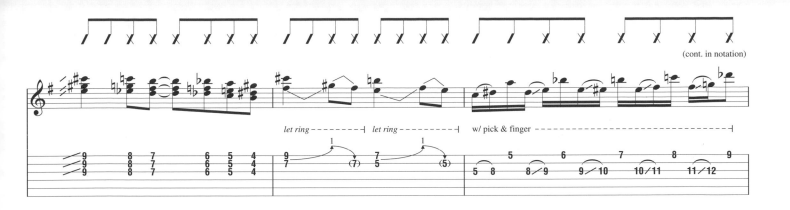

(cont. in notation)

J

Gtr. 1: w/ Rhy. Fig. 3 (3 1/2 times)
Gtr. 2 tacet

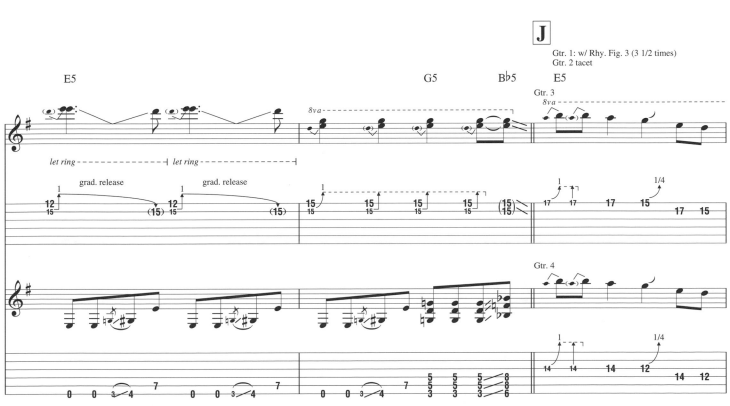

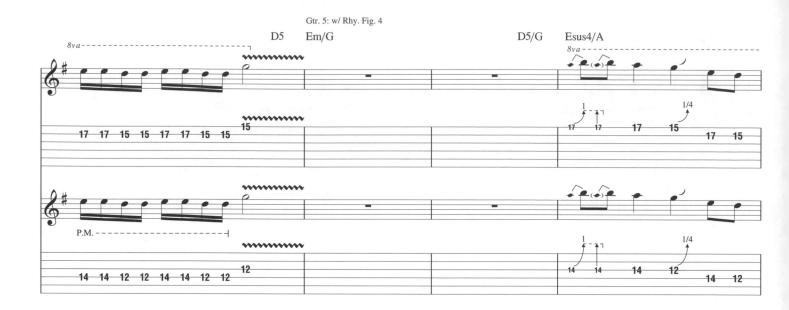

***Bend up while picking sixteenth notes.

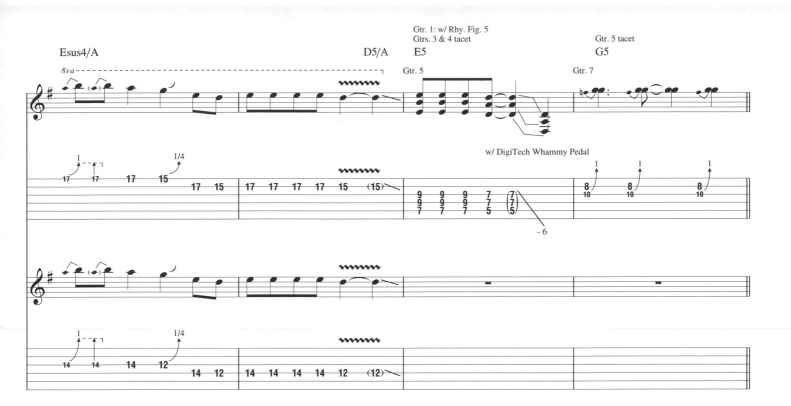

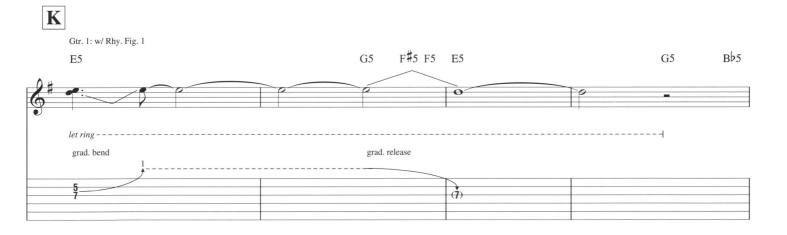

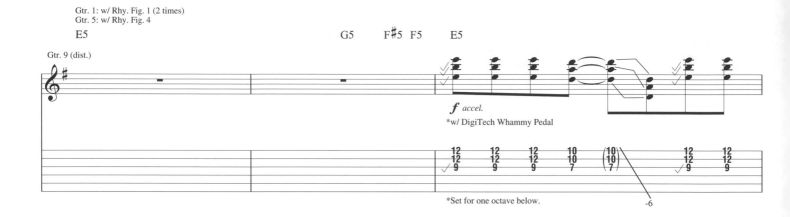

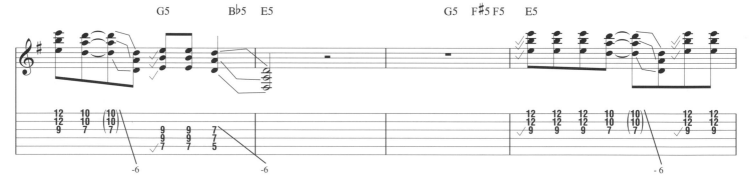

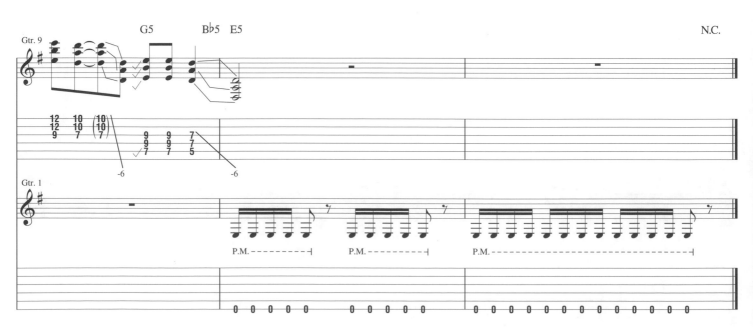

Salt Creek

Music by John 5

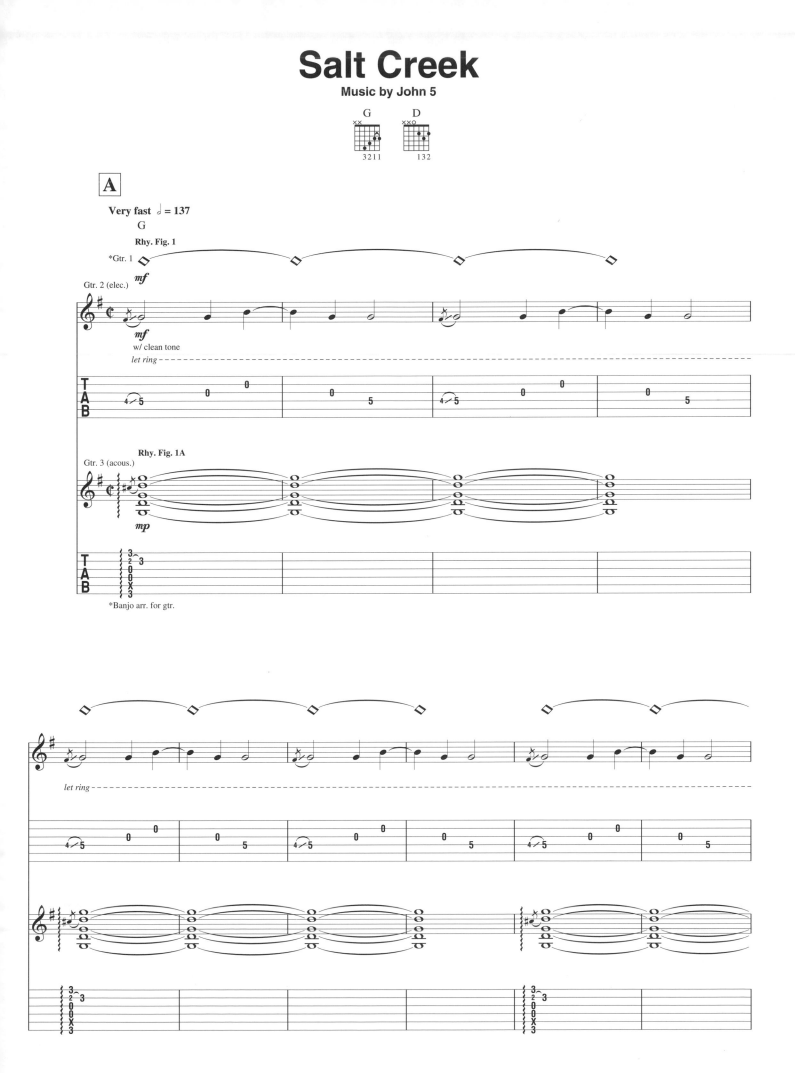

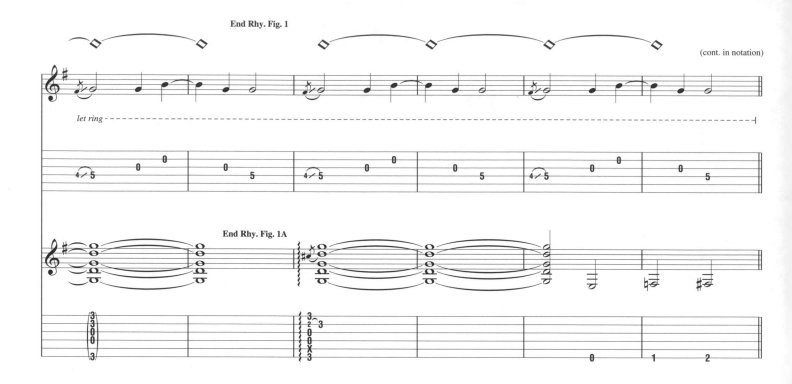

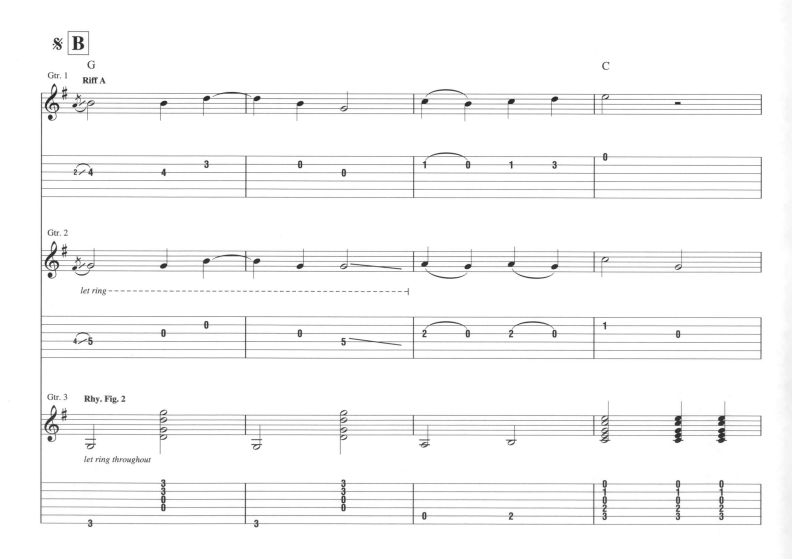

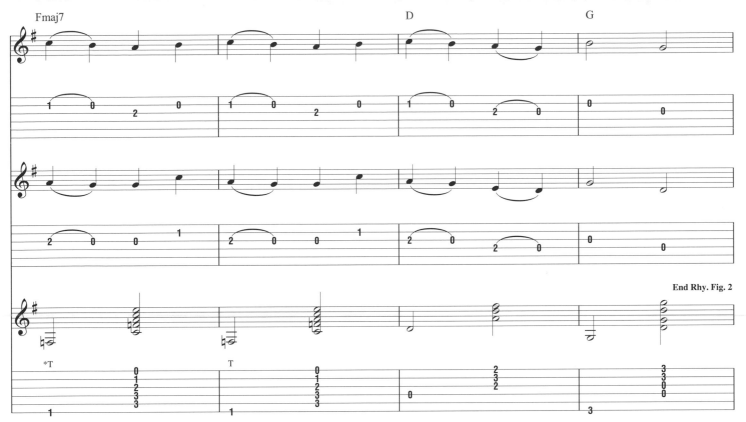

*T = Thumb on 6th string

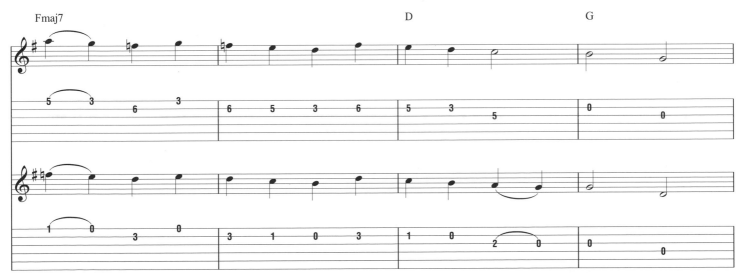

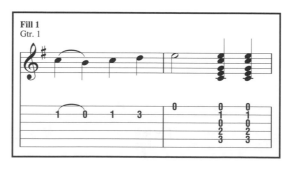

C

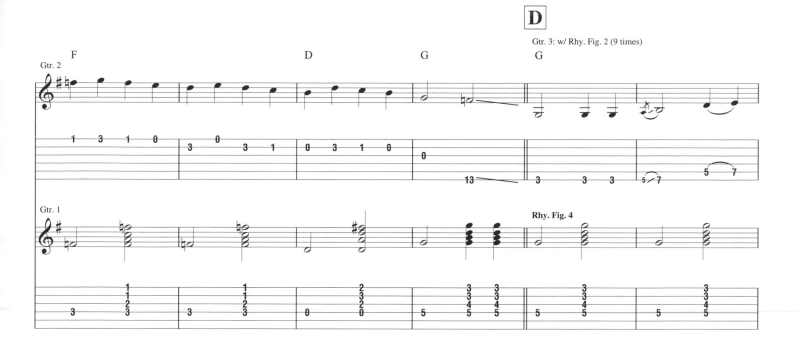

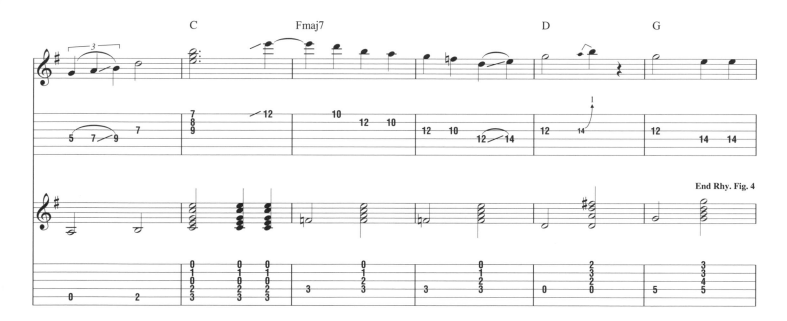

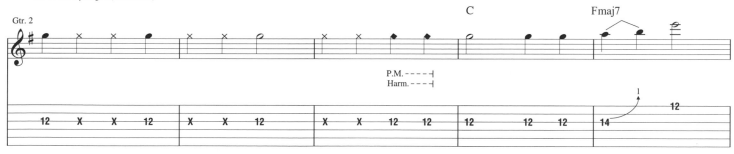

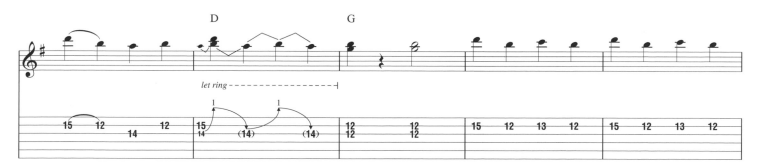

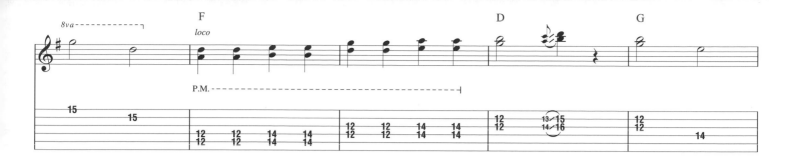

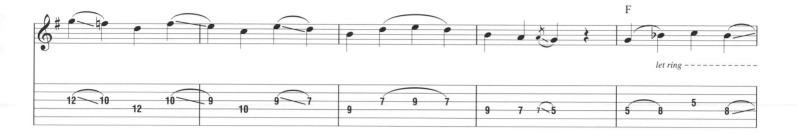

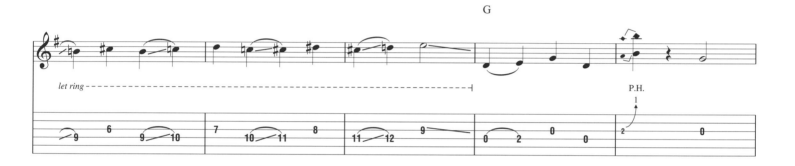

D.S. al Coda 1

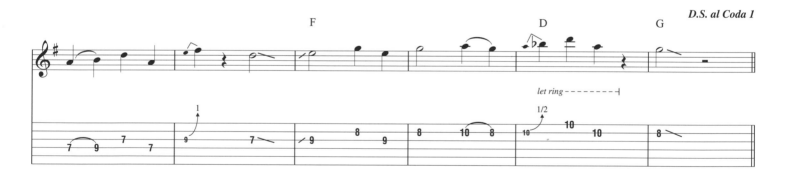

⊕ Coda 1

Gtrs. 1 & 3: w/ Rhy. Figs. 3 & 3A (last 4 meas.)

Gtr. 4: w/ Rhy. Fig. 4 (4 times)
Gtr. 3: w/ Rhy. Fig. 2 (4 times)

F

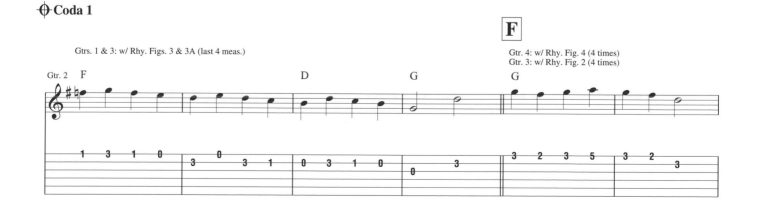

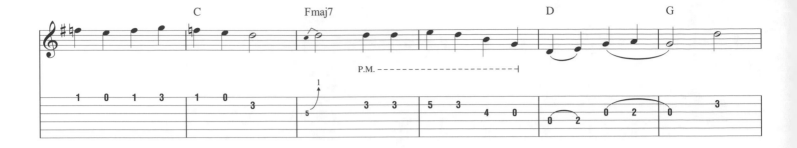

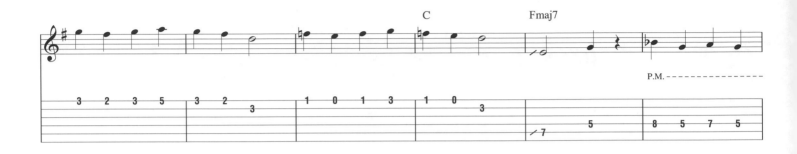

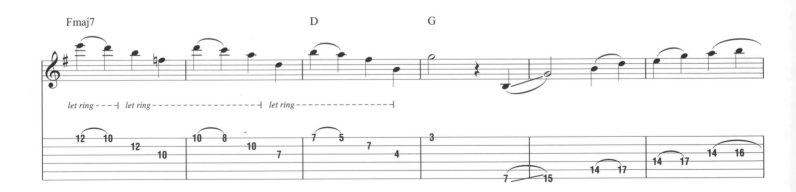

D.S. al Coda 2

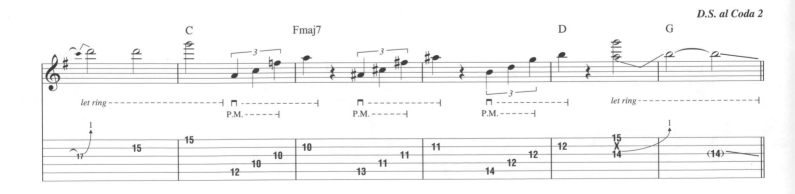

144

Goodnight

Music by John 5

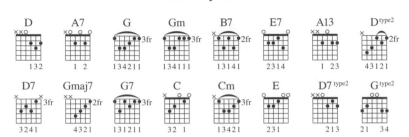

Gtr. 3: Double drop D tuning:
(low to high) D-A-D-G-B-D

A

Moderately fast ♩ = 142

Spoken: Where do we ever get the idea

that in the world of God   it would be a flowery bed of ease?   *I'll tell ya,*

So there, in the will of God can arrest him, throw him in jail. It's midnight, and I'm hurting.

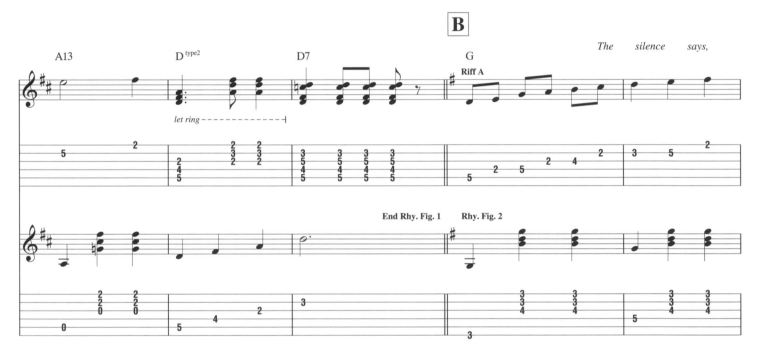

The silence says,

"What are we gonna give him?"   *And the Devil says, "We're gonna give him*

insomnia." "I like your Spanish," he said. If I can't sleep,

the Devil's surely not going to sleep either. Let me tell ya

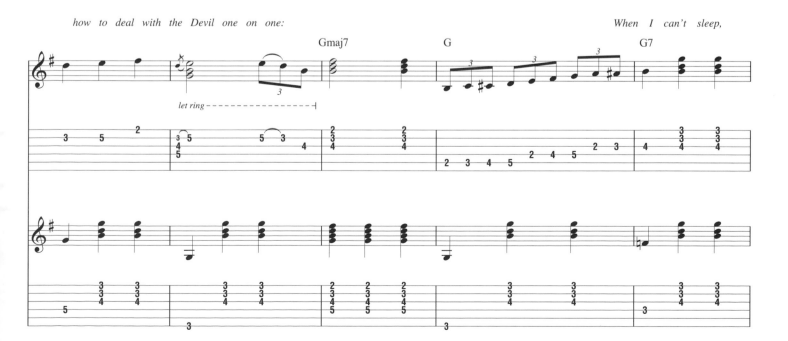

how to deal with the Devil one on one: When I can't sleep,

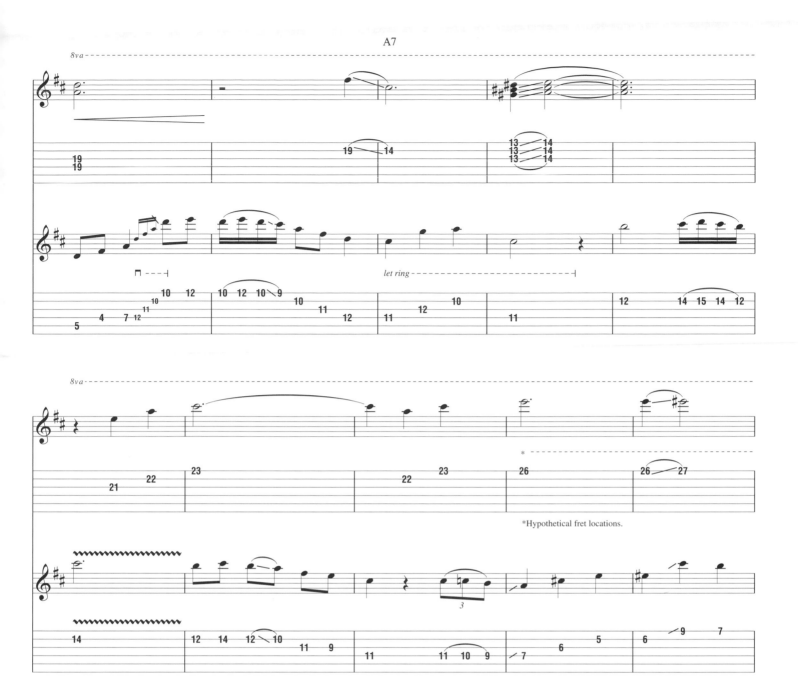

*Hypothetical fret locations.

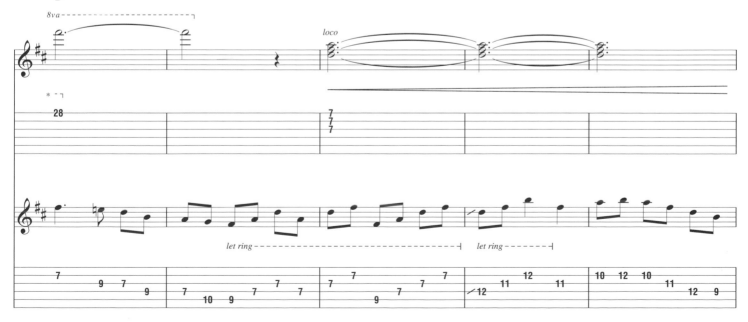

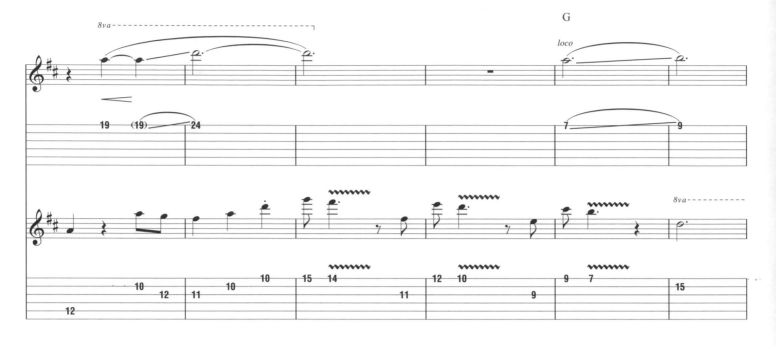

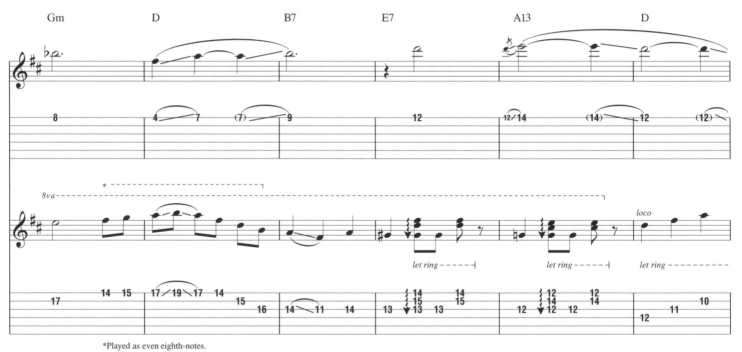

*Played as even eighth-notes.

D

Gtr. 1: w/ Riff A
Gtr. 2: w/ Rhy. Fig. 2

And some will wake up at three in the morning, and you can't

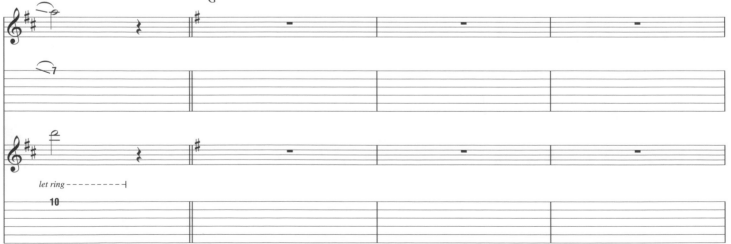

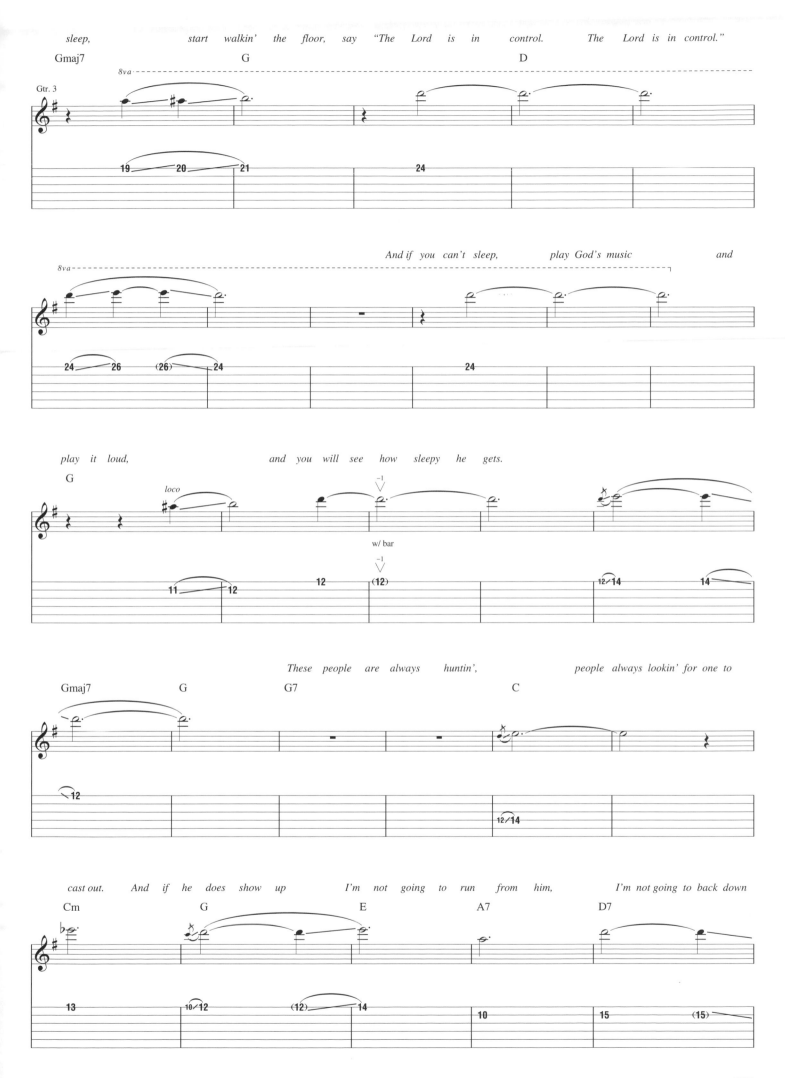

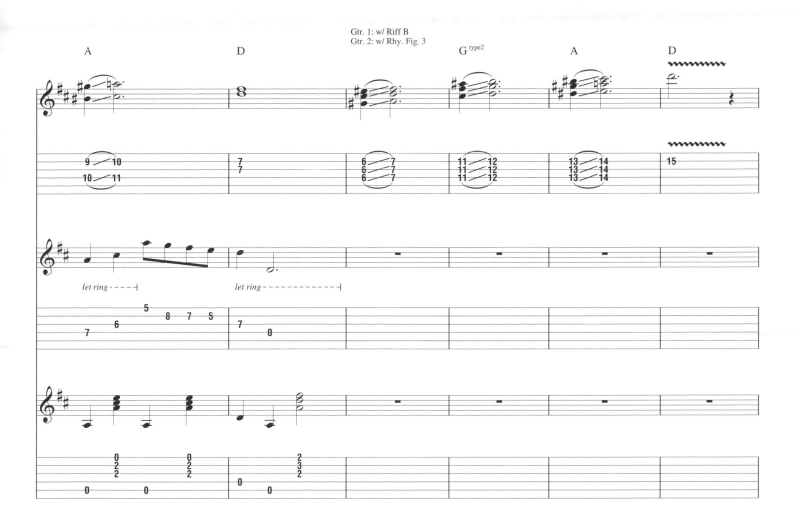

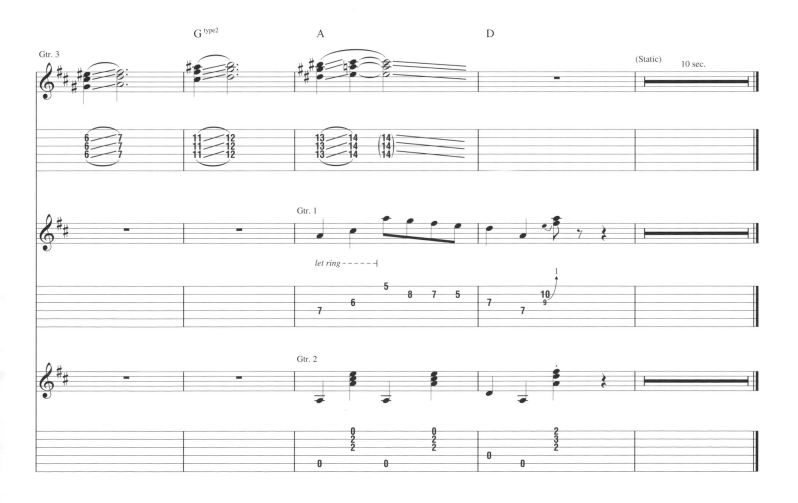

Guitar Notation Legend

Guitar Music can be notated three different ways: on a *musical staff*, in *tablature*, and in *rhythm slashes*.

RHYTHM SLASHES are written above the staff. Strum chords in the rhythm indicated. Use the chord diagrams found at the top of the first page of the transcription for the appropriate chord voicings. Round noteheads indicate single notes.

THE MUSICAL STAFF shows pitches and rhythms and is divided by bar lines into measures. Pitches are named after the first seven letters of the alphabet.

TABLATURE graphically represents the guitar fingerboard. Each horizontal line represents a a string, and each number represents a fret.

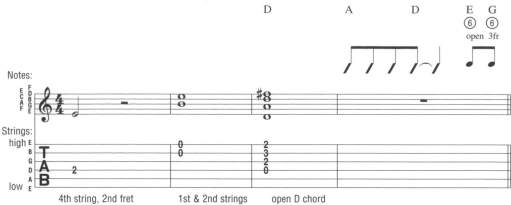

4th string, 2nd fret   1st & 2nd strings open, played together   open D chord

Definitions for Special Guitar Notation

HALF-STEP BEND: Strike the note and bend up 1/2 step.

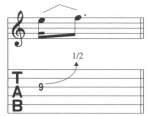

WHOLE-STEP BEND: Strike the note and bend up one step.

GRACE NOTE BEND: Strike the note and immediately bend up as indicated.

SLIGHT (MICROTONE) BEND: Strike the note and bend up 1/4 step.

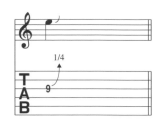

BEND AND RELEASE: Strike the note and bend up as indicated, then release back to the original note. Only the first note is struck.

PRE-BEND: Bend the note as indicated, then strike it.

PRE-BEND AND RELEASE: Bend the note as indicated. Strike it and release the bend back to the original note.

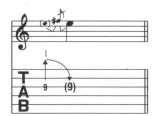

UNISON BEND: Strike the two notes simultaneously and bend the lower note up to the pitch of the higher.

VIBRATO: The string is vibrated by rapidly bending and releasing the note with the fretting hand.

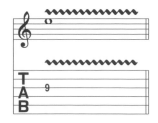

WIDE VIBRATO: The pitch is varied to a greater degree by vibrating with the fretting hand.

HAMMER-ON: Strike the first (lower) note with one finger, then sound the higher note (on the same string) with another finger by fretting it without picking.

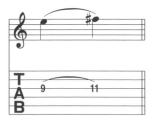

PULL-OFF: Place both fingers on the notes to be sounded. Strike the first note and without picking, pull the finger off to sound the second (lower) note.

LEGATO SLIDE: Strike the first note and then slide the same fret-hand finger up or down to the second note. The second note is not struck.

SHIFT SLIDE: Same as legato slide, except the second note is struck.

TRILL: Very rapidly alternate between the notes indicated by continuously hammering on and pulling off.

TAPPING: Hammer ("tap") the fret indicated with the pick-hand index or middle finger and pull off to the note fretted by the fret hand.

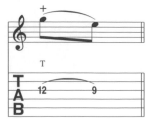

NATURAL HARMONIC: Strike the note while the fret-hand lightly touches the string directly over the fret indicated.

Harm.

PINCH HARMONIC: The note is fretted normally and a harmonic is produced by adding the edge of the thumb or the tip of the index finger of the pick hand to the normal pick attack.

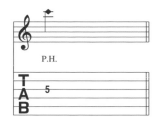

P.H.

HARP HARMONIC: The note is fretted normally and a harmonic is produced by gently resting the pick hand's index finger directly above the indicated fret (in parentheses) while the pick hand's thumb or pick assists by plucking the appropriate string.

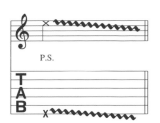

H.H.

PICK SCRAPE: The edge of the pick is rubbed down (or up) the string, producing a scratchy sound.

P.S.

MUFFLED STRINGS: A percussive sound is produced by laying the fret hand across the string(s) without depressing, and striking them with the pick hand.

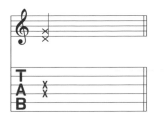

PALM MUTING: The note is partially muted by the pick hand lightly touching the string(s) just before the bridge.

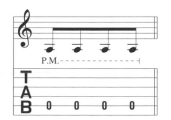

P.M.

RAKE: Drag the pick across the strings indicated with a single motion.

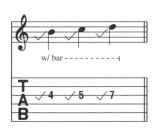

rake- - - -

TREMOLO PICKING: The note is picked as rapidly and continuously as possible.

ARPEGGIATE: Play the notes of the chord indicated by quickly rolling them from bottom to top.

VIBRATO BAR DIVE AND RETURN: The pitch of the note or chord is dropped a specified number of steps (in rhythm) then returned to the original pitch.

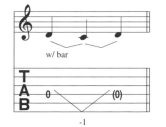

w/ bar

VIBRATO BAR SCOOP: Depress the bar just before striking the note, then quickly release the bar.

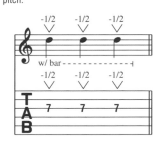

w/ bar - - - - - - - - - -

VIBRATO BAR DIP: Strike the note and then immediately drop a specified number of steps, then release back to the original pitch.

Additional Musical Definitions

>	(accent)	• Accentuate note (play it louder)
^	(accent)	• Accentuate note with great intensity
·	(staccato)	• Play the note short
⊓		• Downstroke
V		• Upstroke

D.S. al Coda   • Go back to the sign (𝄋), then play until the measure marked "*To Coda*," then skip to the section labelled "**Coda**."

D.C. al Fine   • Go back to the beginning of the song and play until the measure marked "*Fine*" (end).

Rhy. Fig.   • Label used to recall a recurring accompaniment pattern (usually chordal).

Riff   • Label used to recall composed, melodic lines (usually single notes) which recur.

Fill   • Label used to identify a brief melodic figure which is to be inserted into the arrangement.

Rhy. Fill   • A chordal version of a Fill.

tacet   • Instrument is silent (drops out).

• Repeat measures between signs.

• When a repeated section has different endings, play the first ending only the first time and the second ending only the second time.

NOTE: Tablature numbers in parentheses mean:
1. The note is being sustained over a system (note in standard notation is tied), or
2. The note is sustained, but a new articulation (such as a hammer-on, pull-off, slide or vibrato begins), or
3. The note is a barely audible "ghost" note (note in standard notation is also in parentheses).

Guitar Recorded Versions

Guitar Recorded Versions® are note-for-note transcriptions of guitar music taken directly off recordings. This series, one of the most popular in print today, features some of the greatest guitar players and groups from blues and rock to country and jazz. Guitar Recorded Versions are transcribed by the best transcribers in the business. Every book contains notes and tablature.

AUTHENTIC TRANSCRIPTIONS WITH NOTES AND TABLATURE

GUITAR PLAY-ALONG

This series will help you play your favorite songs quickly and easily. Just follow the tab and listen to the CD to hear how the guitar should sound, and then play along using the separate backing tracks. Mac or PC users can also slow down the tempo by using the CD in their computer. The melody and lyrics are also included in the book so that you can sing or simply follow along.

INCLUDES TAB

VOL. 1 – ROCK GUITAR 00699570 / $12.95
Day Tripper • Message in a Bottle • Refugee • Shattered • Sunshine of Your Love • Takin' Care of Business • Tush • Walk This Way.

VOL. 2 – ACOUSTIC 00699569 / $12.95
Angie • Behind Blue Eyes • Best of My Love • Blackbird • Dust in the Wind • Layla • Night Moves • Yesterday.

VOL. 3 – HARD ROCK 00699573 / $14.95
Crazy Train • Iron Man • Living After Midnight • Rock You Like a Hurricane • Round and Round • Smoke on the Water • Sweet Child O' Mine • You Really Got Me.

VOL. 4 – POP/ROCK 00699571 / $12.95
Breakdown • Crazy Little Thing Called Love • Hit Me with Your Best Shot • I Want You to Want Me • Lights • R.O.C.K. in the U.S.A. • Summer of '69 • What I Like About You.

VOL. 5 – MODERN ROCK 00699574 / $12.95
Aerials • Alive • Bother • Chop Suey! • Control • Last Resort • Take a Look Around (Theme from "M:I-2") • Wish You Were Here.

VOL. 6 – '90S ROCK 00699572 / $12.95
Are You Gonna Go My Way • Come Out and Play • I'll Stick Around • Know Your Enemy • Man in the Box • Outshined • Smells Like Teen Spirit • Under the Bridge.

VOL. 7 – BLUES GUITAR 00699575 / $12.95
All Your Love (I Miss Loving) • Born Under a Bad Sign • Hide Away • I'm Tore Down • I'm Your Hoochie Coochie Man • Pride and Joy • Sweet Home Chicago • The Thrill Is Gone.

VOL. 8 – ROCK 00699585 / $12.95
All Right Now • Black Magic Woman • Get Back • Hey Joe • Layla • Love Me Two Times • Won't Get Fooled Again • You Really Got Me.

VOL. 9 – PUNK ROCK 00699576 / $12.95
All the Small Things • Fat Lip • Flavor of the Weak • I Feel So • Lifestyles of the Rich and Famous • (So) Tired of Waiting for You • Say It Ain't So • Self Esteem.

VOL. 10 – ACOUSTIC 00699586 / $12.95
Here Comes the Sun • Landslide • The Magic Bus • Norwegian Wood (This Bird Has Flown) • Pink Houses • Space Oddity • Tangled Up in Blue • Tears in Heaven.

VOL. 11 – EARLY ROCK 00699579 / $12.95
Fun, Fun, Fun • Hound Dog • Louie, Louie • No Particular Place to Go • Oh, Pretty Woman • Rock Around the Clock • Under the Boardwalk • Wild Thing.

VOL. 12 – POP/ROCK 00699587 / $12.95
867-5309/Jenny • Every Breath You Take • Money for Nothing • Rebel, Rebel • Run to You • Ticket to Ride • Wonderful Tonight • You Give Love a Bad Name.

VOL. 13 – FOLK ROCK 00699581 / $12.95
Annie's Song • Leaving on a Jet Plane • Suite: Judy Blue Eyes • This Land Is Your Land • Time in a Bottle • Turn! Turn! Turn! • You've Got a Friend • You've Got to Hide Your Love Away.

VOL. 14 – BLUES ROCK 00699582 / $14.95
Blue on Black • Crossfire • Cross Road Blues (Crossroads) • The House Is Rockin' • La Grange • Move It on Over • Roadhouse Blues • Statesboro Blues.

VOL. 15 – R&B 00699583 / $12.95
Ain't Too Proud to Beg • Brick House • Get Ready • I Can't Help Myself • I Got You (I Feel Good) • I Heard It Through the Grapevine • My Girl • Shining Star.

VOL. 16 – JAZZ 00699584 / $12.95
All Blues • Bluesette • Footprints • How Insensitive • Misty • Satin Doll • Stella by Starlight • Tenor Madness.

VOL. 17 – COUNTRY 00699588 / $12.95
Amie • Boot Scootin' Boogie • Chattahoochee • Folsom Prison Blues • Friends in Low Places • Forever and Ever, Amen • T-R-O-U-B-L-E • Workin' Man Blues.

VOL. 18 – ACOUSTIC ROCK 00699577 / $14.95
About a Girl • Breaking the Girl • Drive • Iris • More Than Words • Patience • Silent Lucidity • 3 AM.

VOL. 19 – SOUL 00699578 / $12.95
Get Up (I Feel Like Being) a Sex Machine • Green Onions • In the Midnight Hour • Knock on Wood • Mustang Sally • Respect • (Sittin' On) The Dock of the Bay • Soul Man.

VOL. 20 – ROCKABILLY 00699580 / $12.95
Be-Bop-A-Lula • Blue Suede Shoes • Hello Mary Lou • Little Sister • Mystery Train • Rock This Town • Stray Cat Strut • That'll Be the Day.

VOL. 21 – YULETIDE 00699602 / $12.95
Angels We Have Heard on High • Away in a Manger • Deck the Hall • The First Noel • Go, Tell It on the Mountain • Jingle Bells • Joy to the World • O Little Town of Bethlehem.

VOL. 22 – CHRISTMAS 00699600 / $12.95
The Christmas Song (Chestnuts Roasting on an Open Fire) • Frosty the Snow Man • Happy Xmas (War Is Over) • Here Comes Santa Claus • Jingle-Bell Rock • Merry Christmas, Darling • Rudolph the Red-Nosed Reindeer • Silver Bells.

VOL. 23 – SURF 00699635 / $12.95
Let's Go Trippin' • Out of Limits • Penetration • Pipeline • Surf City • Surfin' U.S.A. • Walk Don't Run • The Wedge.

VOL. 24 – ERIC CLAPTON 00699649 / $14.95
Badge • Bell Bottom Blues • Change the World • Cocaine • Key to the Highway • Lay Down Sally • White Room • Wonderful Tonight.

VOL. 25 – LENNON & MCCARTNEY 00699642 / $14.95
Back in the U.S.S.R. • Drive My Car • Get Back • A Hard Day's Night • I Feel Fine • Paperback Writer • Revolution • Ticket to Ride.

VOL. 26 – ELVIS PRESLEY 00699643 / $14.95
All Shook Up • Blue Suede Shoes • Don't Be Cruel • Heartbreak Hotel • Hound Dog • Jailhouse Rock • Little Sister • Mystery Train.

VOL. 27 – DAVID LEE ROTH 00699645 / $14.95
Ain't Talkin' 'Bout Love • Dance the Night Away • Just Like Paradise • A Lil' Ain't Enough • Panama • Runnin' with the Devil • Unchained • Yankee Rose.

VOL. 28 – GREG KOCH 00699646 / $14.95
Chief's Blues • Death of a Bassman • Dylan the Villain • The Grip • Holy Grail • Spank It • Tonus Diabolicus • Zoiks.

VOL. 29 – BOB SEGER 00699647 / $14.95
Against the Wind • Betty Lou's Gettin' Out Tonight • Hollywood Nights • Mainstreet • Night Moves • Old Time Rock & Roll • Rock and Roll Never Forgets • Still the Same.

VOL. 30 – KISS 00699644 / $14.95
Cold Gin • Detroit Rock City • Deuce • Firehouse • Heaven's on Fire • Love Gun • Rock and Roll All Nite • Shock Me.

VOL. 31 – CHRISTMAS HITS 00699652 / $12.95
Blue Christmas • Do You Hear What I Hear • Happy Holiday • I Saw Mommy Kissing Santa Claus • I'll Be Home for Christmas • Let It Snow! Let It Snow! Let It Snow! • Little Saint Nick • Snowfall.

VOL. 32 – THE OFFSPRING 00699653 / $14
Come Out and Play • Gotta Get Away • Hit That • Million M Away • Original Prankster • Pretty Fly (For a White Guy) • Esteem • She's Got Issues.

VOL. 33 – ACOUSTIC CLASSICS 00699656 / $12
Across the Universe • Babe, I'm Gonna Leave You • Crazy on • Heart of Gold • Hotel California • Running on Faith • Thick a Brick • Wanted Dead or Alive.

VOL. 34 – CLASSIC ROCK 00699658 / $12
Aqualung • Born to Be Wild • The Boys Are Back in Town • Bro Eyed Girl • Reeling in the Years • Rock'n Me • Rocky Mount Way • Sweet Emotion.

VOL. 35 – HAIR METAL 00699660 / $12
Decadence Dance • Don't Treat Me Bad • Down Boys • Sevent • Shake Me • Up All Night • Wait • Your Mama Don't Dance.

VOL. 36 – SOUTHERN ROCK 00699661 / $12
Can't You See • Flirtin' with Disaster • Hold on Loosely • Jessic Mississippi Queen • Ramblin' Man • Sweet Home Alabam What's Your Name.

VOL. 37 – ACOUSTIC METAL 00699662 / $12
Fly to the Angels • Hole Hearted • I'll Never Let You Go • Lov on the Way • Love of a Lifetime • To Be with You • What You • When the Children Cry.

VOL. 38 – BLUES 00699663 / $12
As the Years Go Passing By • Boom Boom • Cold Shot • Every I Have the Blues • Frosty • Further On up the Road • Killing Fl • Texas Flood.

VOL. 39 – '80S METAL 00699664 / $12
Bark at the Moon • Big City Nights • Breaking the Chains • Cul Personality • Lay It Down • Livin' on a Prayer • Panama • Smol in the Boys Room.

VOL. 40 – INCUBUS 00699668 / $14
Are You In? • Drive • Megalomaniac • Nice to Know You • Par Me • Stellar • Talk Shows on Mute • Wish You Were Here.

VOL. 41 – ERIC CLAPTON 00699669 / $12
After Midnight • Can't Find My Way Home • Forever Man • I S the Sheriff • I'm Tore Down • Pretending • Running on Faith Tears in Heaven.

VOL. 42 – CHART HITS 00699670 / $12
Are You Gonna Be My Girl • Heaven • Here Without You • I Bel in a Thing Called Love • Just Like You • Last Train Home • T Love • Until the Day I Die.

VOL. 43 – LYNYRD SKYNYRD 00699681 / $14
Don't Ask Me No Questions • Free Bird • Gimme Three Steps Know a Little • Saturday Night Special • Sweet Home Alabam That Smell • You Got That Right.

Prices, contents, and availability subject to change without notic